RUCKSACK GUIDE
Winter Mountaineering

ALUN RICHARDSON

ILLUSTRATED BY GEORGE MANLEY

A&C BLACK • LONDON

Published by A & C Black Publishers Ltd
36 Soho Square, London W1D 3QY
www.acblack.com

Copyright © 2009 Alun Richardson

ISBN 978 0 7136 8680 7

A CIP catalogue record for this book is available from the British Library.

Acknowledgements
Cover photograph © Alun Richardson
Inside photographs © Alun Richardson
   except pp. 12, 39, 41 Clive Hebblethwaite; p. 28 istockphoto.com;
   p. 35 Shaun Hutson; p. 4 Kenneth G. Libbrecht and pp. 88, 107
   Steve Long
Illustrations by © George Manley, except p. 6 © Crown Copyright
(2008), the Met Office
Designed by James Watson
Edited by Lucy Beevor

Typeset in 9/10pt Din-Light by Margaret Brain, UK

Printed and bound in China by C&C Offset Printing Co., Ltd.

The ideas in this book are the culmination of 25 years mountaineering and time spent discussing techniques with inspirational climbers, Mountain Guides and instructors, in particular Alan Dance, Dave Williams, Steve Lewis, Graeme Ettle, Bruce Goodlad, Eric Pirie, Trevor Massiah, Jim Beynon, Clive Hebblethwaite, John Taylor, Twid Turner, Louise Thomas, Pat Littlejohn and Matt Spencely.

Special thanks to Lesley Jones who supported me throughout; Clive Hebblethwaite who supplied some of the photographs; Adam Gent who assisted with the weather sections; Rhiannon Richardson and Molly Jones for help with text and diagrams; George Manley for his excellent illustrations; Robert Foss and Lucy Beevor from A&C Black; and the manufacturers who generously supported the photo shoots: DMM, Lyon Equipment, Mountain Equipment, Face West, Select Solar, Mammut and Fritschi.

Any of the opinions expressed in this book are mine alone and should not be associated with any of the above people, companies or organisations.

Winter Mountaineering is the fourth book in the **Rucksack Guide** series and covers the skills required to become a competent winter mountaineer. This handy book can be kept in your rucksack and will help you to gain the experience to mountaineer safely in winter anywhere in the world. It does not cover the technical aspects of navigation or alpinism (see **Rucksack Guides** to *Mountain Walking and Trekking* and *Alpinism*).

The **Rucksack Guide** series tells you *what* to do in a situation, but it does not always explain *why*. If you want more information behind the decisions in these books, go to *Mountaineering: The Essential Skills for Mountaineers and Climbers* by Alun Richardson (A&C Black, 2008).

For more information about the author, his photographs and the courses he runs go to:

www.freedomphotographs.co.uk or
www.alunrichardson.co.uk.

On a cold clear day, with firm snow, winter mountaineering can be safer than in summer. However, it can all change in a few hours and gale force winds, blizzards, zero visibility, avalanches and the numbing cold will soon sap your reserves.

Winter starts as the Sun drops on the horizon and the Earth is warmed less effectively. In the Northern Hemisphere this allows the Polar Front to move south bringing colder air from the Arctic. From autumn, through winter and well into spring, the battle between the warmer moist air to the south, and the colder drier air to the north, produces the winter storms that bring the snow to the UK and North America. (See *Mountaineering: The Essential Skills for Mountaineers and Climbers* (A&C Black, 2008) or *Rucksack Guide: Mountain Walking and Trekking* (A&C Black, 2009) both by the author, for more information on how our weather is made).

The low pressure gradient within winter storms often creates strong winds of 160kph plus. Gusts of 70kph and above are difficult to walk in and the wind above 800m, especially in Scotland, is at least double the strength at sea level. The wind chill factor can make it feel even colder: +5°C in a 50kph wind can feel like –12°C on exposed flesh. The mountains in winter are serious places.

EXPERT TIP

Alun Richardson
IFMGA/BMG Guide
www.freedomphotographs.co.uk

'Don't let blind ambition ruin your winter trip. The mountains will always be there – will you?'

Aanoch Eagach traverse, Glencoe, Scotland

SNOW AND ICE

When the temperature of a cloud falls below 0°C, tiny particles, such as bits of clay, encourage water to turn into ice crystals that then combine to form snowflakes.

A snowflake is a number of snow crystals that join together as they fall through air that is close to freezing. When the temperature is ideal for stickiness, and the wind is light enough not to break them up, the flakes can grow very large.

Varying temperature, moisture and wind conditions favour crystal growth in different ways (Fig. 1):

- **Stellar crystals (1)** The classic star-shaped snowflake
- **Columns (2)** New snow crystals in a six-sided hollow or solid prism
- **Needles (3)** Long, thin forms
- **Plates (4)** Thin, usually hexagonal crystals
- **Graupel** Soft hail created by water droplets that freeze to crystals forming round particles
- **Ice pellets** Form when rain falls though a very cold air mass

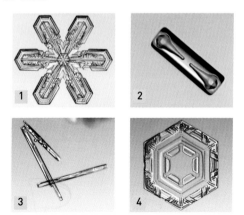

Fig. 1 Snow crystal formations

There are two ways air can rise in winter:

FRONTAL LIFT

When warm, moist air is lifted over cold air it cools, forming clouds, rain or snow. The warmer the air, the more moisture it contains, and the faster it rises and cools, the greater the snowfall. Therefore, air masses originating in warmer areas, such as the Atlantic and the Pacific Oceans, have a tendency for greater snowfall.

However, just because a cloud contains snow does not mean it will land as snow – rain, freezing rain, sleet and snow can all fall on the same place as the front moves overhead.

- When warm air extends to ground level, the snow melts and falls as rain (most winter rain is actually melted snow).
- If the band of cold air is relatively thin and the ground is below freezing, the falling rain cools and turns into ice when it hits something, causing freezing rain.
- When the layer of cold air is thick enough, the falling rain freezes into ice pellets. If the snow can fall all, or most, of the way through cold air, it falls as snow. At very cold temperatures snowflakes do not form and the snow mostly comprises snow crystals.
- If the snowflakes fall and rise again, they can melt and refreeze forming hailstones.
- Sleet is a soft melted snowflake that has refrozen.

OROGRAPHIC LIFT

Although frontal lifting is the major cause of summer storms, in winter the mountains themselves have a major effect. As a storm front, or even just moist air, reaches the mountains it is forced upwards (orographic lift). The resulting cooling can then form snow. The rate of lifting depends on the steepness of the mountains and is greater when the air mass hits the mountain range straight on.

To identify possible snowstorms, look for the path of the depression and its associated fronts:

- What is its origin? Does it contain moisture?

- Is it travelling over cold areas and can it pick up moisture?

- Is the air dry and cold? Since water vapour is needed to make clouds and snow, cold air will tend to produce lighter snow than warmer air, which is why a years' worth of snow at the South Pole melts down to less than 8cm of water. In general, the heaviest snow usually falls when the temperature is only a little below freezing, or even above freezing at ground level.

- Is the air mass hitting the mountains straight on?

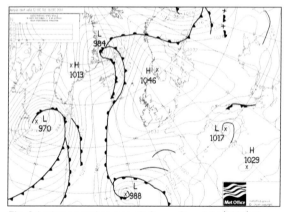

Fig. 2 *A winter weather map, © Crown Copyright (2008), the Met Office. In this example the UK is experiencing sunshine and light winds from an anticyclone. A developing polar low north of Iceland will bring cold polar air and some snow from the moisture it picks up over the sea.*

COLD CLEAR SPELLS

High pressure established over Northern Europe or the US during winter can bring a spell of cold easterly or northerly air streams to the UK or US. The clear skies, settled conditions and light winds associated with high pressure allow heat to be lost from the surface of the Earth. The temperature then falls overnight, leading to air or ground frosts. Fog can also form, because the winds are light.

SNOWPACK CHANGES

Snow on the ground undergoes cycles of change (metamorphism), unless it is −40°C or less. Ice (from crystal surfaces) changes into water vapour, which moves through the snowpack from warm to colder areas and is deposited as ice on other grain surfaces. Water vapour also moves at the crystal level from the points to the hollows so that the points become blunt and the hollows fill, affecting the structure and stability of the snowpack.

The difference in temperature from the bottom to the top of the snowpack – and more importantly in individual layers – dictates the rate of vapour transfer and is called the temperature gradient (Fig. 3, overleaf). The temperature at ground level is always 0°C, which means that the lower the air temperature and the thinner the layer or snowpack, the greater the temperature gradient.

- Anything between 5°C and 10°C/m is a moderate gradient.
- Anything below 5°C/m is a weak gradient.

The depth of snow, aspect of the slope and the air temperature all affect the temperature gradient. Strong temperature gradients promote greater vapour movement than weak gradients. Extreme temperature gradients of 50–60°C/m over short sections of the snowpack are not uncommon in Scotland.

The changes in the snowpack do not occur in isolation and are complicated by further snowfall. This results in layering of the snowpack, with the associated danger of avalanches.

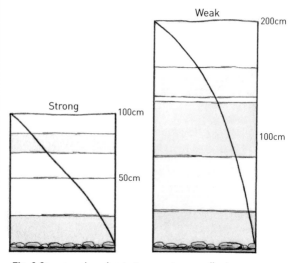

Fig. 3 Strong and moderate temperature gradients throughout the snowpack – a large temperature gradient promotes faceting; a weak temperature gradient promotes rounding.

If the temperature gradient is weak, usually when the outside temperatures are moderate or the snowpack is deep, the rounding process (equilibrium metamorphism) dominates (Fig. 4). Rounding breaks down the snow crystals and stabilises the snowpack. Close to 0°C the change is rapid and the snow layers consolidate and become denser, stronger and more stable in a relatively short period of time.

DETECTING ROUNDING

To assess when the snow has become stable, consider how quickly rounding is taking place. Tony Daffern (*Avalanche Safety for Skiers and Climbers*, 1999) states that small sluffs from steep ground and snow falling off trees may be indicators that rounding is taking place, but there are exceptions to every rule! The weight of further snowfall speeds up the stabilisation of the lower layers.

Fig. 4 The process of rounding

In a strong temperature gradient the faceting process (kinetic metamorphism) dominates, where rounded snow crystals are transformed into angular shaped crystals or facets (Fig. 5). These crystals do not bond well to each other and form weak layers. Since the snowpack is usually warmer near the ground and colder towards the surface, the vapour moves from crystals in the lower layers to crystals in the layers above. If this process continues, the crystals will develop into a cup-shaped crystal called 'depth hoar'.

THE DANGERS
Faceting is faster when the snowpack is loose and there are crusts present, which stop the vapour escaping. Faceted grains and depth hoar can persist for a long time and cause cycles of avalanche activity for the rest of the winter and even into the spring or, in some cases, summer. According to *Avalanche Accidents in Canada* (Geldsetzer & Jamieson, 1999), faceted grains and surface hoar are the weak layers in the failure plane in 78 per cent of fatal accidents.

Fig. 5 The process of faceting. The final part of the process leads to 'depth hoar' (far right).

If the snowpack melts and refreezes during the night, water evaporates from the snowpack and the grains of snow fuse to form larger grains, to the point where water (from surface melting, rain and ground water drainage) can percolate through the snow. This can form loosely packed granular grains called 'sugar' or 'corn' snow. The water can also lubricate layers adjacent to the ground and cause wet slab avalanches. A warm, dry wind rapidly accelerates the loss of water from the snowpack and the formation of sugar snow.

Fig. 6 *A slab avalanche. Avalanches can occur wherever there is snow on the ground.*

Fig. 7 *Cornices collapse when they get heavy (Aanoch Mor, Scotland).*

- **Cornices** An overhanging mass of snow formed on the lee sides of ridges by wind action.
- **Corn snow** Coarse, round crystals formed when surface layers melt and refreeze for several days.
- **Crust** Forms when melted water on the surface freezes. If the source of heat is the Sun it is called Sun crust.
- **Powder snow** Light, fluffy, newly fallen snow.

Fig. 8 *Nieves penitents*

- **Nieves penitents** A tall, sometimes curving column of ice or compacted snow found at high altitudes and created by deep Sun cups (p.14). So-called because it resembles someone kneeling in prayer (Fig. 8).
- **Rime (hoar in Scotland)** A weak, dull, white, dense deposit formed by super-cooled water droplets freezing on objects exposed to the wind (Fig. 9).

Fig. 9 *Rime builds in the direction of the wind (see above). In this case, the wind blew from the left to the right.*

Fig. 10 Wave-like sastrugi

- **Sastrugi** When wind erodes the snow it leaves a variety of shapes, such as wave-like sastrugi (Fig. 10).
- **Sun cups** A pit in a snowfield that resembles a cup and is caused by differential melting as the Sun moves. They can become very deep when dirt trapped in the hollows absorbs more heat.
- **Surface or hoar frost** Forms on the surface of the snow when there is a clear sky with high humidity and little or no wind. These crystals sparkle on trees and on the snow surface after a clear, cold night. Once buried under a new snow layer they can be difficult to detect and very dangerous.

If the ground is dry and cold, not much ice will form. A series of melt freezes are required to release water. Because snow melts more easily than ice, the next freeze will make the ice grow, but the snows disappear.

TYPES OF ICE

Type	Description
Water ice	Melt freeze of hard firn or neve snow. The best ice to climb, but rarely forms on steep cliffs above 70 degrees.
Blue ice	More dense and watery, developed from water drainage and snowfall, which sticks to it, giving it its plastic nature.
Water ice	Icicles from water flow. Transparent, hard and brittle.
Verglass	Formed by freezing rain or freezing of surface trickles. It is rock hard.
Ice crust	Melt freeze of surface snow. Very brittle.

Fig. 11 *Point Five Gully, Scotland*

Experienced winter mountaineers seem to have an instinctive feeling for avalanche conditions. In reality they are combining their knowledge of the previous day's weather, and the information from the avalanche report, with the conditions they meet when climbing. This expertise is only achieved by experiencing winter in all its guises, but there are some basic principles that will help.

Each time snow falls, or is blown by the wind, it creates a new layer. After the snow has landed each layer undergoes changes caused by temperature, wind and pressure. This results in different types of avalanche (Fig. 12).

Fig. 12 Avalanche categories

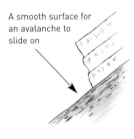

A smooth surface for an avalanche to slide on

A full-depth avalanche occurs when the whole snow cover slides on to the ground (*see* sideview, right).

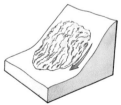

A flowing wet avalanche. Whether an avalanche is defined as wet or dry will depend on the moisture content.

A surface avalanche occurs when one layer slides on to another.

An airborne powder avalanche occurs when it reaches 65kph (40.4mph).

A loose snow avalanche starts from a single point.

A slab avalanche occurs when an area of more bonded snow slides off the weaker surface below (see sideview, right).

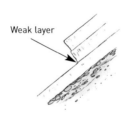

Weak layer

REDUCING YOUR CHANCES OF BEING CAUGHT

- Avalanches occur whenever snow is lying on a slope of sufficient angle, but mostly at 30–45 degrees.

- It does not have to be snowing for slopes to become avalanche prone (see faceting, p.10).

- Ninety per cent of the time victims or members of their party trigger avalanches.

- It is not just large slopes and amounts of snow that should concern you; small patches of snow on a climb or ridge can slide, taking you with them. A small depth of snow in a large gully can slide creating a lot of snow at the bottom of the gully.

WHAT CREATES AVALANCHE CONDITIONS?

The weather is the most important factor. It deposits new snow, creates the wind that can redistribute the snow on to new slopes and, combined with temperature fluctuations and gravity, it causes the changes in the snowpack.

- **Effects of temperature** See metamorphism (p.11).

- **Effects of wind** Even on a clear day, with no snowfall, the wind can rapidly redistribute snow on to lee slopes forming wind slab. A warm wind can also stabilise other slopes by aiding evaporation. When wind blows over the top of a mountain the leeward side experiences top-loading. When the wind blows over a ridge that leads up the mountain it may cause cross-loading. The effects of cross-loading are subtle, usually more difficult to spot and tend to be less stable.

- **Heavy snowfall** Eighty per cent of avalanches happen during, or soon after, heavy snowfall, due to the extra weight of fresh snow and the difference between its consistency and the layer below. Snow falling at 2–3cm per hour, or more, rapidly increases avalanche danger.

- **Rain** In the short term rain can cause instability through additional loading and possible lubrication of lower layers, but when the snowpack refreezes it can also help to stabilise it (see melt freeze metamorphism (p.11) and rounding (p.9)).

AT HOME

Use the previous day's weather to predict the amount of snow that may have fallen, where the wind may have redistributed it and whether it is thawing. Look at the avalanche report, but remember it is a prediction made by experts in previous days and should be adapted according to the conditions you meet on the mountain.

SNOW AND AVALANCHE REPORT LOCHABER

AVALANCHE HAZARD 1500 HRS THU 1/3/07
Overnight the freezing level dropped and frequent snow showers
were blown on a North-Westerly wind. This has deposited large
areas of windslab on East to South aspects above 1000m. This
windslab shows moderate bonding. The avalanche hazard is
Considerable (Category 3). An avalanche crown wall was noted on
an Easterly aspect at an altitude of 1200m (Easy Gully on Aonach
Mor).

AVALANCHE HAZARD OUTLOOK FRI 2/3/07
Southerly winds will strengthen through Friday. This will begin to
re-deposit the existing windslab from Southerly and Easterly
aspects to Northerly aspects. Snow during Friday afternoon and
evening will also deposit windslab on Northerly aspects. Areas of
unstable windslab will be found in many sheltered locations on
North-West through East to South aspects above 1000m.
Avalanches are likely to occur on steep slopes and gullies where
deep deposits of this unstable windslab are located. The avalanche
hazard will be Considerable (Category 3).

CLIMBING CONDITIONS
SNOW DISTRIBUTION: Fresh snow above 700m.
ICING: Improving in colder temperatures.
COMMENT: Southerly winds strengthening during Friday.

For more information on conditions, please visit our Blog http://saislochaber.blogspot.com

Fig. 13 Remember; an avalanche report is a prediction made
by experts in previous days – you must make your own
assessment on the hill.

FROM THE VALLEY

As soon as you leave your car you should start
questioning the predictions you made at home.

- Can you see avalanche activity, especially on slopes
  with the same aspect as those on your journey?
- From what direction has the wind been blowing?
- Can you see the current wind direction from snow
  being blown from the ridges? Where is the snow
  accumulating?

- Are slopes loaded with fresh or drifted snow? How much has it snowed (80 per cent of all avalanches occur during or shortly after a storm)? More than 2cm/hr of new snow can produce unstable conditions and more than 30cm continuous snow is very hazardous.

DURING THE WALK/CLIMB

- Continue to look for signs of where the wind is/has been blowing – is it a local wind created by the mountain and different to the weather forecast?
- Look for sastrugi (Fig. 10) or parallel etching where the steep edge faces the direction from where the wind was blowing, and rime (Fig. 9), which builds in the direction of the wind. Look for cornice build-up.
- Feel for changes in the consistency of the snow under foot. Settling of the snowpack is due to the presence of slab – the harder the slab the more it will settle. Hard slab is harder than wind crust, does not sparkle, and the surface has a velvety texture and a dull, matte colour. Are small slabs releasing easily as you cross small safe slopes?
- Is there a sudden temperature rise? Is the Sun just catching the top of the crag? Carry a thermometer on your rucksack to spot temperature inversions.
- Do you feel unsafe? The gut instinct of the experienced mountaineer should not be underestimated; it usually means your subconscious has spotted something.

AVALANCHE DANGER SCALE

American and European avalanche danger scales are similar, with the exception that they use slightly different colours (see Appendix, pp. 131–2).

You can travel in the mountains without ever standing on a potential avalanche slope by choosing a route that keeps to gentle slopes or defined ridges and avoids lee slopes, plateau rims and open slopes. When choosing where to travel consider the following.

WHAT IS THE ANGLE OF THE SLOPE?

Most large slab avalanches occur on slopes between 30 and 45 degrees, but this statistic may be misleading because these are the angles that most walkers and skiers travel on. Snow will not stick easily to slopes above 60 degrees, but unstable slopes just below this may therefore release very easily, so take care approaching climbs.

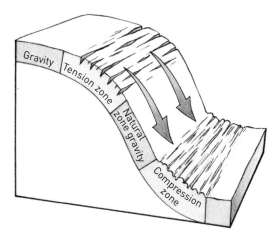

Fig. 14 *Convex slopes are most hazardous because the point of maximum convexity is a frequent site of tension fracture.*

AVALANCHES

Fig. 15 *Wind and snow blowing off the ridge can indicate where slab avalanches are likely to be forming.*

WHAT SURFACE IS THE SNOW RESTING ON?
Smooth ground is more likely to result in full-depth avalanches, whereas rough ground, or large boulders, will tend to anchor the base layers in position. However, once the boulders are covered, a surface avalanche can continue unhindered. Large trees and rocks that stick up through the snowpack can help to hold it in place.

WHAT IS THE SLOPE'S ORIENTATION TO THE SUN?
- North-facing slopes receive little or no Sun, stay cold and can extend the period of avalanche danger.
- South-facing slopes are warmer, but can develop thin crusts that increase the chances of weak layers.
- East-facing slopes catch the Sun in the colder morning, and therefore melt slowly.
- West-facing slopes catch the Sun in the warmer afternoon.

During cloudy conditions there will be very little difference between sunny and shady slopes.

CORNICES

A collapsing cornice can trigger some avalanches. They can be collapsed by the weight of climbers or when warm weather or rain makes them denser. Avoid climbing below cornices during a heavy thaw or sudden temperature rise, and 24–48 hours after snowstorms or heavy drifting. Also take care walking above them (Fig. 16).

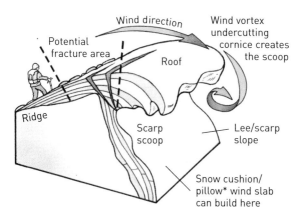

Fig. 16 *The fracture line on a cornice is a long way from the edge, which can be very dangerous.*

*Snow cushion/pillow A snowdrift on a slope, often within the starting zone of an avalanche, which looks like a cushion or pillow.

WHAT IS THE SLOPE'S ORIENTATION TO THE WIND?

- Lee slopes, including the sheltered side of ridges and plateau rims, become loaded with snow after a storm or heavy drifting.

- The crests of mountain ridges are safer – they are usually protected from avalanches, and ribs and buttresses provide rock belays to provide security. However, even small avalanches can take you off your feet and down a cliff on to steeper ground. Travel on the windward side of ridges to avoid wind-blown snow and cornices.

- Gullies (couloirs) are natural accumulation zones for slabs and should be avoided when the avalanche risk is high or it is thawing and cornice collapse is possible.

- Look above you – it is often these slopes that are triggered, which then swoop down on to the slope you are on. Avalanches from ice routes above can pour down on an otherwise seemingly safe ice climb.

- Beware of blind faith; tracks on the slope do not mean it is safe, even if you crossed it safely earlier in the day.

Fig. 17 The wind is the most important factor in the creation of slab avalanches.

Suspect slopes can be partially evaluated by digging a snow pit on smaller safe slopes of similar orientation and altitude to the main slope (extrapolate for situations higher up, where surface slab layers may be much thicker). Analysing a slope is not an exact science and even experts get it wrong. If you are unsure it may be better to select a different route.

- Dig several pits, rather than analyse one in depth.
- Use an avalanche probe to find a representative place with average depth. Dig a snow pit 1m wide and down to the first thick layer of old refrozen snow, or 1.5–2m deep (no deeper, because it is rare for humans to trigger avalanches deeper than this).
- Smooth the vertical back wall of the pit, feeling for any changes, and then probe with a finger or fist all the way down to assess the hardness of the layers (see overleaf).
- Look for the weakest layer and try to estimate how well it is bonded to adjacent layers.

HARDNESS OF THE SNOW

1 is hard, 5 is soft

- **5** Gloved fist penetrates
- **4** Four gloved fingers penetrate
- **3** One gloved finger penetrates
- **2** Pick of an ice axe penetrates
- **1** Knife penetrates

AVALANCHES

If you find any of the following, it may be a dangerous weakness in the snowpack:

- Adjacent layers of differing hardness
- Very soft layers (fist penetrates easily)
- Water drops squeezed out of a snowball made from any layer
- Layers of ice
- Layers of graupel, which act like a layer of ball bearings
- Feathery or faceted crystals
- Layers of ice or loose, un-cohesive grains
- Air space.

You should also make a judgement about bonding within the layer. Is it going to break up easily? Is the whole layer bonded and will the whole slope slide?

SHOVEL TEST

The shovel test judges the cohesiveness of the layers (Fig. 18). It must be practiced over years, to the point where you build up a feeling for the relative stability of layers – most beginners tend to overrate the danger.

A potential problem of the test is that you are removing the weight of snow from the layer each time you dig and it is difficult to assess the influence of this factor. Because of the small sample size, you need to do several tests to get a true feel for the snow's stability.

- Having made the snow pit observations, isolate a wedge-shaped block, cutting down to the top of the next identified layer.
- Cut behind the column to below a suspect layer (not the whole column).
- Insert the shovel behind and pull straight out; don't lever on the shovel. Do this for each suspect layer.

- Look for smooth, straight shears that pop out. Try to rank them as easy, moderate, hard etc.
- If a block slides off during cutting, there is obviously a weak layer. If the block slides off with pressure from the shovel – and it must be a clean smooth shear to mean anything – and there is 15cm or more snow on top, turn each block upside down to see which weak layer was involved.

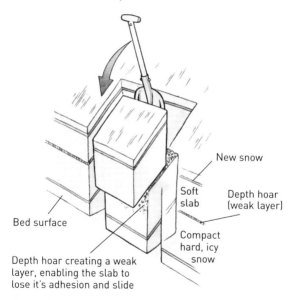

New snow

Soft slab

Depth hoar (weak layer)

Bed surface

Compact hard, icy snow

Depth hoar creating a weak layer, enabling the slab to lose it's adhesion and slide

Fig. 18 *The cohesiveness of the layers can be judged using the shovel test.*

QUICK PITS

As you climb, dig snow stances, cut steps or create a belay. Make a quick check on the surface layers with your ice axe.

It is rarely essential to negotiate an avalanche-prone slope, but if you do have to proceed consider the following:

- Belay someone down the slope to check it out. Are you going to be swept over a cliff or will an avalanche pile up at the bottom?
- What will happen should the slope avalanche, i.e. is the snow bonded?
- What is the depth of snow?
- Is it likely to be a slab or loose snow avalanche?
- Zip up, wrap a scarf round your mouth and nose and wear a hat.
- Take your hands out of any leashes on poles and ice axes.
- Carry avalanche transceivers, a probe and a shovel.
- Direct descent or ascent of a potential avalanche slope is safer than traversing.
- Cross or descend one at a time in the same track – the rest of the party should watch closely.
- Beware that it is possible to trigger avalanches from below a suspect slope.

Fig. 19 An avalanche close to Mt Everest Base Camp

If the unthinkable happens, fight for your life! If you are not close to the surface and you have not created an air space your chances of survival are slim.

- Delay the avalanche taking you by plunging your axe into the snow. This may help to keep you near the top of the slide.
- Shout.
- Run to the side, or jump up-slope above the fracture.
- If the slab is hard, try to remain on top of a block.
- Get rid of poles, but recent evidence does suggest that wearing a rucksack increases your surface area and keeps you higher in the avalanche.
- Try to roll like a log off the debris.
- Swimming motions are rumoured to help.
- As the avalanche slows make a desperate effort to get to the surface, or at least get a hand through.
- Push the snow away from your face and try to maintain an air space.
- Take and hold a deep breath at the last moment to maintain space for chest expansion.
- Try to avoid panic and conserve your energy. Your companions will be searching for you.

EXPERT TIP

Blyth Wright
SAIS Co-ordinator
Co-ordinator@SAIS.gov.uk

'All the world's avalanche forecasts in two websites:

www.sais.gov.uk
www.avalanche-center.org'

AVALANCHES

A buried victim has an 80 per cent chance of survival if they have an air space, are no deeper than 2m and they are located within 15 minutes (see *Rucksack Guide: Ski Mountaineering* for searching with an avalanche transceiver). Survival chances decline to 40 per cent after 1 hour and 20 per cent the hour after that. Someone buried under more than 2m of snow has an almost zero chance of survival.

● Check for further avalanche danger and post a look-out.
● Mark the point of entry and the point where the victim was last seen.
● Make a quick search of the debris, looking for signs and sounds.
● Probe the most likely burial spots – pay particular attention to shallow depressions in the slope and around rocks and trees.
● Make a systematic search, probing the debris with axes or poles.
● Send for help.
● Do not give up – the longest someone has survived is 22 hours.

Fig. 20 *Digging for an avalanche victim. Mountain walkers rarely carry avalanche transceivers, shovels and probes, yet digging with your hands is slow and strenuous.*

AVALANCHES

- 'Avalanches can be triggered by shouting.'
  Avalanches cannot be triggered by most sounds, because any forces exerted in sound waves are far too low. The very large shockwaves produced by explosions can trigger avalanches, however, if they are close enough to the surface.

- 'Avalanches strike without warning.'
  Avalanche conditions usually give obvious signs. The process of creating avalanche conditions begins many hours – or even days – before.

- 'If you make it across a suspect slope without it avalanching, it is safe.'
  All that it tells you is that you did not load it enough to release an avalanche.

- 'Avalanches only happen during storms.'
  Storms only bring the snow; what happens in the snowpack to create avalanche conditions depends on many factors.

- 'Waiting 2–3 days after storms is safe.'
  Avalanche conditions can occur whenever there is a slope and snow. Wind can create avalanche conditions on an otherwise sunny day by redistributing snow.

- 'If there are tracks then the slope is safe.'
  This may be, but it may also be because the previous climbers did not load the slope enough to trigger an avalanche.

- 'The slope has never been known to slide, so it's safe.'
  Unless its less than 25 degrees, the slope has the potential to avalanche.

- 'Transceivers keep you safe.'
  All transceivers do is enable your rescuers to locate you – whether you are alive is another matter.

- 'There is not enough snow to avalanche.'
  Snow can slide on any surface and early season full-depth avalanches are common.

The cold and wind makes winter mountaineering extremely serious.

Hypothermia is the lowering of the body's core temperature and is exacerbated by cold air, wet clothing, tiredness, low energy levels and dehydration. Prevention is better than cure, so eat, drink, wear layers and stay dry.

SYMPTOMS

Hypothermic people do not generally notice the symptoms so it is important for others in the group to spot the signs. Hypothermia affects people in different ways and no one symptom is reliable, but the following can be indications:

- Feeling cold.
- Mild shivering and cold hands or feet do not indicate you are hypothermic, but that your body is trying to generate heat to warm you.
- Uncontrolled shivering means that you are hypothermic.
- A lack of shivering does not mean you are not hypothermic, since this can be a symptom of severe hypothermia.
- Cold hands and feet indicate your body is fighting the cold by reducing the flow of blood to the extremities to maintain the body's core temperature.
- Muscles are stiff, weak and less responsive.
- Mental disorientation, inappropriate behaviour and slurred speech, which means that accidents are more likely.
- Armpit feels cold.

HYPOTHERMIA SYMPTOMS

Type	Symptoms
Mild hypothermia	• Uncontrollable shivering • Loss of coordination or slurring of words
Severe hypothermia	• A further deterioration of mental status to unresponsiveness • The trunk will feel cold to the touch and the body may be rigid • In severe cases, pulse and respiration may be absent, but the patient should not be considered dead until re-warming has been accomplished.

TREATMENT

- Stop and warm the person, put them in dry clothes and a hat and protect them from the elements and further heat loss.

- Put them in a sleeping bag protected from the ground (having someone else in the bag may not be as beneficial as previously thought).

- The skin warms up before the core, so the victim may feel better before they are ready to move.

- Exercise will not help, because at this stage they have depleted their energy reserves so much that they cannot even shiver.

All winter climbers suffer from numb feet or hands, maybe for hours at a time, with no ill effects. It is important, however, to realise that below −10°C any tissue that feels numb for more than a few minutes can become frozen. It rarely occurs above −10°C without wind chill.

FROST NIP

In the early stages of frostbite (frost nip), in the unthawed state, the skin is yellow-grey, painless, numb and leathery to the touch. If you feel numbness in your extremities and the temperature is low, flex your fingers and toes, stamp your feet, clap your hands or place them somewhere warm such as your armpits or groin. This will bring feeling back to the limbs, accompanied by painful 'hot aches' or 'screaming barfies' as the warm blood defrosts the nerve endings. It can be reversed if treated in time.

DEEP FROSTBITE

In deep frostbite the tissue is hard, white and obviously frozen. It can be stabilised, but will not heal properly until you have sought medical help. It is better to move for six hours with frozen feet to a place of safety than to thaw the feet at a high camp, as walking on vulnerable inflamed thawed tissue will result in further damage.

Treatment

If you cannot reach medical help, once you have reached safety start to re-warm the limbs by immersion in hot water (39–42°C – about as hot as an elbow can stand) for periods of 20 minutes, moving fingers and toes if possible. Do not knock or rub the frozen tissue. Avoid smoking (nicotine contracts blood vessels), but alcohol may be helpful (it dilates blood vessels), but only when the victim is not hypothermic.

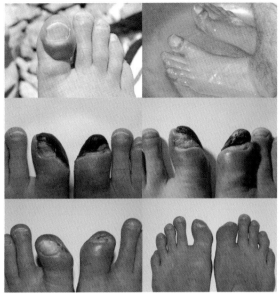

Fig. 21 *The development of frostbite at 30 hours; 4 days; 35 days; 75 days; 178 days (post-op); and 250 days.*

- By far the most important treatment after re-warming is to keep the skin as clean as possible to avoid any infection.
- Separate fingers and toes and wrap them in clean bandages.
- The victim must not use the thawed tissue, which may require them to be fed and even helped to use the toilet.
- If a hot water container is not available, warm the affected parts in a warm sleeping bag (or on the abdomen, groin or armpits) for several hours.
- Give oxygen if available.

WARNING

Frostbite can be avoided, even at extremes of altitude, temperature and fatigue. Keep your limbs dry, wear adequate clothing, carry spare gloves and dry socks, and don't wear your boots too tight. Carelessness is often a major factor, as is becoming dehydrated. Smoking and caffeine do not help.

Several hours after thawing the tissue swells, and during the first two days giant blisters form. Do not puncture them; they will settle during the first week leaving tissue that is discoloured, and possibly gangrenous, shrunken and black. If the frostbite is superficial, new pink skin will appear beneath the discoloured tissue. If it is deep, the end of the toe or finger gradually falls off – an unsightly, but usually painless, process. It is difficult to predict the outcome in the first few weeks after frostbite, and remarkable recoveries do occur. Surgery is usually best avoided, until it is clear that there is no other alternative.

EXPERT TIP

Shaun Hutson
shaun@sphutson.com

'Just because you have had very cold feet and hands in oxygen-rich lower altitudes without frostbite, don't think you can apply the same approach to higher altitudes. Frostbite is often the result of ignoring a bit of the body.'

WINTER ROUTE FINDING

If your navigation skills need refreshing see *Rucksack Guide: Mountain Walking and Trekking*. The skills for navigating in winter are the same as for navigating in summer, but the weather is worse; it is cold, gloves get in the way, the daylight hours are shorter, and avalanches and cornices must be avoided. Walking on a bearing and pacing must be spot on, because there are fewer features and you may even be crawling on your hands and knees!

Carry a spare map, compass, and a reliable head torch with a spare torch or batteries and bulbs. A 1:50,000 map can sometimes be better for winter navigation, because the detailed landscape features shown on a 1:25,000 map are often obscured by snow. However, a 1:25,000 map shows more detail for complex route finding. It also makes it easier to take accurate bearings.

When conditions are difficult it is important to have a robust strategy and use more obvious features:

- Add notes inside your map case, with crucial compass bearings, distances, altitudes, pacing and timings for each navigation leg.
- Use linear features, but beware that new fences, ski tows, etc. can confuse the issue.
- Sometimes in intermittent poor visibility it may be easier to follow features that are hazardous, such as a cliff edge, where cornices may be impossible to see. If you do take these routes, rope-up at a safe distance (15–20m) and walk parallel to, but away from, the edge.
- Understand attack points and aiming off.
- Mentally 'tick off' obvious features as you pass them, and think carefully about collecting features for when you overshoot.
- Beware of following footprints; they are a morale booster but should be abandoned if their direction does not fit the compass bearing.

- Be careful near streams, trees and boulders, as you can break through the snow.
- Accurate timing is difficult to do in winter, because of the fluctuating snow conditions, but still use it to tell you when you may have walked too far.
- Pacing is also difficult when the snow conditions are changeable. You should understand what is happening to the ground and always relate it to your pacing.
- Slope aspect removes whole sections of the hillside where you are not. Throw snowballs down the slope; this should help you to identify the fall line...if they disappear, stop!
- Do not navigate too complicated areas – instead, head for obvious changes in slope direction and angle.

Fig. 22 *The skills are the same as summer navigation, but the conditions may be much worse.*

Whiteout occurs when the horizon and the ground merge into one due to cloud and snow. Add strong winds and darkness, and it can be a frightening and bewildering experience. Distances, slope angles, directions and speeds become more difficult to judge.

To stay calm, plan your route, identify hazards, measure compass bearings and write them down from the comfort of a bothy bag. If you do change your plan, write it down so you can match the ground to the map or backtrack later.

It is easy to drift off your bearing, especially in a strong wind or when following a sloping traverse where there is always the tendency to drift downhill. To avoid this:

● Send one person following a bearing, in front of the main navigator.

● As the lead person begins to drift to the left or the right, the navigator can shout instructions to bring them back on course.

● Use an altimeter and GPS if you have one, but remember strong winds can affect the altimeter and cliffs can cause errors in the GPS signal.

Fig. 23 It is easy to drift off your bearings in strong winds.

OUTRIGGERS

A useful method for finding narrow valleys is to walk in line as if conducting a sweep search, with the main navigator in the middle. A relative rise or fall in the heads indicates the shape of your slope, e.g. at the bottom of a narrow valley the people either side will be above the navigator.

Fig. 24 Always carry anti-fog goggles in a rigid case (to avoid scratching or breaking). They are invaluable when trying to map read and navigate with hail being flung at your face.

A 2003 review showed that of over a thousand rescues in Scotland, navigation, bad planning and poor timing were the three biggest causes of accidents. Another factor identified was different aspirations and abilities within groups, leading to poor decisions. Good planning combined with observations on the hill will help to make a great and safer winter day in the mountains.

- Get the current and previous days' weather forecast and avalanche report to plan where you are going.
- Prepare food and drink and pack your rucksack the night before.
- Let someone know where you are going. The effectiveness of mountain rescue teams is improved if a description of your plans is available.

CHOOSING A GOOD ROUTE

Good snow conditions make travelling in the mountains faster and safer, while poor snow makes it frustrating and dangerous. If you are heading out in poor conditions, as is often the case in Scotland, the danger can be minimised by choosing a good route before going out. Draw arrows on the map showing the prevailing weather conditions to help you determine potential avalanche-prone slopes, deep snow and cornices.

- Think about the direction of the Sun – in the Northern Hemisphere, south and west slopes catch the afternoon Sun and consolidate more quickly.
- Dirty snow consolidates more quickly than clean snow.
- Beware of hidden holes next to trees and rocks.
- Ridges are not the place to be in a storm. They are, however, a good choice when the snow is deep or avalanches have been predicted.
- Do not be afraid to turn back.

South Gully, Creag Meagaidh, Scotland, climber J. Husband.

Returning late or being benighted do not justify alerting the voluntary mountain rescue services. Things do go wrong, so be prepared to spend the night out at least once in your winter mountaineering career.

Snow holes vary from one dug for survival to one in which you can spend several nights or even weeks. They are stronger in a storm than tents or a bivvy bag, which must be continually dug out. They are also less cold than outside and quieter. Find somewhere free of avalanche danger, such as snow-drifts in rivers (but take care not to fall through) and near ridges. Arrange the entrance so that it is on the leeward side of a slope to give protection from the wind, but beware, as more snow will gather there during the night.

DIGGING THE HOLE

- It is difficult to dig a snow hole with an ice axe, so if you plan to snow hole carry a small metal shovel that is the same size as your rucksack.

- To lessen the chances of breaking your shovel keep the shaft short and do not lever back on the handle.

- Digging is a wet and tiring job so wear full waterproofs, but remove layers so that you have a dry set for when you finish.

- Rotate the work to avoid either of you becoming too hot or too cold.

- An insulating mat will keep your knees warm and a plastic bivvy bag makes it easier to pull snow from inside the shelter.

- The softer the snow, the thicker the walls need to be.
- A plastic sheet on the interior floor is useful.
- Keep a shovel inside if you need to dig snow out.
- Mark the exterior with wands or blocks so that you do not step through the roof of the shelter.
- Smooth the inner walls to stop drips.
- Take care cooking or using candles, as ventilation is usually poor. Poke a ventilation hole with a ski stick and shake it every so often to keep the hole open.

Fig. 25 Digging a snow hole is wet work, so take a few layers off and put waterproofs on (mountaineer D. Williams).

SURVIVAL SHELTER

- In an emergency, dig into a snow bank or a drift to create a compartment large enough for you to at least sit upright.
- Sit on ropes or your rucksack or, using the pad from it, loosen your boots and put your feet into the rucksack.
- When you cannot find a slope to dig into, dig a trench deep enough and long enough for you to lie in comfortably.
- Line the bottom with insulating material.
- Use ski poles for the roof, covering them with a bivvy bag and loose snow or blocks of hard pack snow.
- Dig a tunnel in from the side and plug it with snow.

1

Fig. 26 Three survival shelters.

SNOW CAVE

This is just a larger survival shelter with more thought and work put into it. Dig the entrance so that the door is below the sitting level.

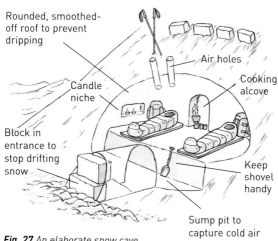

Rounded, smoothed-off roof to prevent dripping

Air holes

Candle niche

Cooking alcove

Block in entrance to stop drifting snow

Keep shovel handy

Sump pit to capture cold air

Fig. 27 An elaborate snow cave

The secret to enjoying winter mountaineering and ice climbing is to pay attention to the simple things, such as removing metal piercings, and adjusting your layers to climb cool and belay warm. Try to stay dry at all costs, even if it means moving more slowly! Long pitches can save time, but when the weather is nasty or cold, shorter pitches will help to keep everyone warmer.

Staying warm also depends on maintaining your energy levels. Eat a big breakfast and snack every 30 minutes. Slow-burning carbohydrates such as peanut butter, jam or honey sandwiches work well. Use rapid energy gel packets when it is very cold. Do not smoke and consume plenty of fluids, because dehydration causes the capillaries in the fingers to shut down.

Carry a jet boil stove or Thermos. To make your Thermos go further, fill your mug with packed snow and melt it with the warm drink.

Fig. 28 The excellent Jet Boil stove. A warm drink is only psychologically different to a cold one; it is the drink's energy content that keeps you warm.

- A base layer and mid-layer fleece with a waterproof over the top is usually enough when walking. Vary them to reduce sweating.

- Change into a dry base layer when you reach your climb or part-way through the day.

- Carry extra warm clothing for when you stop moving and put an extra layer on before you are really cold.

- Ensure that there is enough room to move in your waterproof jacket and trousers or salopettes, or you put another layer on underneath (although they should not be too loose, as cold air exchanges easily with the warm air inside).

- Cuffs and openings should be easy to adjust with gloves on and must keep the snow out.

- A large hood which fits over your helmet or hat is essential. All zip toggles must be large enough to grab with gloves on.

- Legs radiate less heat and sweat less, so good, well-fitting trousers are important. A popular option is to wear long johns underneath a thinner pair of trousers.

- When you are wearing a harness, removing your waterproof to add a layer is a problem – try layering on top with a synthetic high-loft insulated jacket (belay jacket) such as the Mountain Equipment Trango jacket.

PROTECTING YOUR HANDS

- Keep your core temperature up and your hands dry (do not put wet hands into gloves).

- The wrist has the third highest heat loss of the body, so ensure your layers are long enough, and make some fleece wrist-overs.

- Carry a waterproof shell glove or mitt and lots of thin and thick gloves with sticky palms.

- Change gloves whenever they are wet and your hands cold (a new pair for every pitch when climbing).
- Avoid gloves with a floating liner, because they are difficult to get on and off.
- Carry a pair of fleece mitts that are easily accessible at belays and for when it is really cold.
- Attach gloves to your wrist with a keeper cord.
- If you are doing a lot of walking with your hand on top of your axe, consider taping a piece of thin closed-cell foam over the top.
- Do not grip your ski poles or axe handle too tightly and keep your hands out of the loops.
- Keep emergency 'hand warmer' packets for putting in gloves, and even your boots, or carry a charcoal warmer in your pocket.
- Do not blow on your fingers or into your gloves, as this makes them damp.

Foam

Use tape to secure foam

Fig. 29 Tape thin closed-cell foam over the top of your ice axe to protect you from the cold.

KEEPING YOUR HEAD WARM

Wear a fleece hat, balaclava or even a neoprene beanie under your helmet. A fleece neck gaiter or a fleece jacket with a hood will seal your neck and prevent heat loss during long belays.

KEEPING YOUR BODY WARM

LOOKING AFTER YOUR FEET

Feet have little muscle bulk and it is much easier to keep them warm than to warm them up.

- On long belays, avoid standing on snow, weight your feet equally and stamp your feet when they start to chill.
- Try to minimise the body closing down the extremities by dressing according to the route and climate, and don't scrimp on leg protection.
- Keep your feet dry, even if it means changing your socks during the day.
- Wear gaiters.
- Foot powder with aluminium hydroxide can help to reduce perspiration.

For information on vapour barrier liners see *Rucksack Guide: Mountaineering in Remote Areas of the World* (A&C Black, 2009).

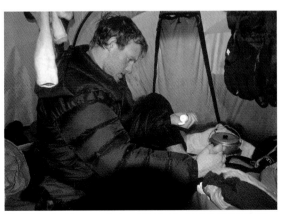

Fig. 30 *Look after your feet and toes, or you risk losing them (Gareth Richardson).*

Boots suitable for winter use will have room for your toes to wriggle, be stiffer and have a sharp edge to the sole for edging in snow.

BOOT TYPES

Type	Pro	Con
Leather boots	• Good for climbing mixed routes in less-than Arctic conditions • Provide a more precise feel	• Not as warm • Less waterproof
Plastic boots	• Provide warmth • Provide good support for ice climbing • Waterproof	• Mostly heavier • Less sensitive • The shells cover two size ranges, with a thicker inner to pad out the smaller size (this collapses over time)

To make the issue of boot/crampon compatibility more straightforward, boots and crampons can be graded according to their basic design and intended use. However, not all manufacturers follow the system designed by Scarpa (Fig. 32, p.55).

BOOT COMPATIBILITY
Graded B0 to B3, dependent on the stiffness of the sole and the support provided by the uppers:

- **B0** Flexible walking boots. Any boot that can be bent more than half an inch when standing on the front edge will be less suitable for use with all crampon types.

- **B1** Stiff mountain walking boots suitable only for occasional use with C1 crampons.

- **B2** Very stiff mountaineering boots suitable only for use with C1 or C2 crampons.
- **B3** Fully rigid, winter climbing and mountaineering boots suitable for use with C1, C2 or C3 crampons.

Fig. 31 *A sturdy pair of boots with room for your toes to wriggle is essential for warmth and stability on snow.*

Crampons and boots make an integral unit – using the wrong type of crampons on the wrong type of boots can break them or cause them to fall off the boot. Crampons are graded C1 to C3, depending on their attachment method and flexibility. When buying crampons, always take your boots with you and fit the crampons in the store.

CRAMPON COMPATIBILITY

- **C1** Lightweight articulated or flexible walking crampons with simple straps. Most commonly 10 point (2 front and 8 bottom). They are light, simple and a good choice for occasional use (low-angle snow, glacier crossing).

- **C2** Articulated or flexible step-in crampons attached with a heel clip and toe strap. Most commonly 12 point (4 front and 8 bottom). Give the best balance between ease of attachment, walking comfort and climbing performance. A good choice for general mountaineering and low- to mid-grade climbs.

- **C3** Stiffer, or even fully rigid, crampons attached with a heel clip and toe bail. They usually have 12 or more points, and adjustable front points (mono or dual). The best choice for pure ice and climbing performance, but take some getting used to for general mountaineering/ walking.

FRONT POINTS

- Front points should stick out by 25–35mm.

- Front points that are drooped and the second row angled forward are more suited to ice climbing. The angled second points reduce calf strain by resting against the ice.

- Downward-facing second points facilitate a more ergonomic walking motion.

TERRAIN	CRAMPON			BOOT		
Low-level walking	C1	C2		B1	B2	B3
Mountaineering						
Snow routes Grades 1–2						
Snow routes Grade 3 up			C3			
Buttress climbing						
Mixed climbing and ice-fall climbing						

Fig. 32 Crampon/boot compatibility table

- Horizontal front points are more versatile and work better than vertical ones for pure ice climbing (two are better than one).
- Vertical front points tend to come out of the ice easier when the heel is raised. However, vertical mono points do provide more precision and are the best choice for very steep, hard ice and mixed ground. If the route is predominantly firm snow or ice, stick with two.

Fig. 33 A good general mountaineering crampon will do a better job on waterfall ice than a waterfall ice crampon will do in the mountains.

SHARPENING CRAMPON POINTS

- Sharpen the points with a hand file, not a grinder – the heat generated makes the points brittle.
- For moderate mountaineering, sharpen front points once a season and leave the rest of the points as they are.
- For harder routes, the sharpness and length of your front and secondary points is more important.
- A modular design crampon allows you to replace just the front points.
- Vertical technical points need not be razor sharp like a pick, but should have a point, so you can stand on the smallest edges.

TIPS FOR FITTING AND USING CRAMPONS

- The sole of your boot should match the shape of the crampon, without any large gaps.
- A correctly adjusted crampon should remain attached to the boot with the straps and clips undone.
- Put crampons in a crampon bag and carry them inside your pack.
- Trim the straps to a sensible length (long, dangling straps can catch on the other crampon), but allow enough length to attach gaiters.
- Check all boots and screws are tight, that straps are not cut or damaged, and that there are no cracks in the linking bar or crampon.
- If you forget anti-balling plates, use a plastic bag and tape, but do not expect it to last for very long.
- Carry some plastic ties, a strap, some cord and a small nut and bolt to repair crampons.

CRAMPON ATTACHMENT
There are three attachment systems:

1 **Strap on** Useful in exceptional circumstances, e.g. for high altitude boots, but they have been superceded by a plastic heel cup and plastic front bail found on most C1 crampons. They will fit on boots without a heel and toe lip.

2 **Step-in** A wire toe bail fits over the welt and a heel tension lever snaps into place on the heel. The system typically includes an ankle strap. It's a secure system for plastic boots and leather boots with soles that have deep notches on toes and heels. Correctly fitted, these are fast, vibration free and easy to use but, for most climbers, a mixed binding is better, because they are easier to put on when your boots are iced up and safer as the welt wears down.

3 **Mixed** Simple, efficient and suitable for most uses, except steep waterfall ice climbs. The heel attaches with a lever and the toes attach with a strap and a ring or a plastic bail. They can be used with lighter mountaineering boots, without heavy welts.

Fig. 34 *Anti-balling plates are essential to prevent the build-up of snow on the underside of crampons, especially in wet snow conditions. The traditional remedy is to tap your crampons with your ice axe, but this is awkward, time consuming and distracting.*

RUCKSACK

- A 45–55 litre simple tube rucksack with a lid or pocket and compression straps is big enough.
- Avoid crampon pockets, side pockets and ice axe tubes etc., because they add weight and can get caught on everything when climbing.
- A removeable, padded lightweight waist belt is best for climbing.

EYE PROTECTION

Snow reflects a lot of the Sun; even when it is not shining. Take sunglasses and goggles for navigating in a blizzard.

HELMET

Ensure your balaclava or fleece hat can fit underneath your helmet and that it has an attachment for a head torch. A classic style helmet may be better than a foam one, because of the increased risk of falling ice.

HARNESS

Ensure your harness fits over all of your clothing and that you can go to the toilet wearing it.

SKI POLES

Ski poles are better than an ice axe on easy-angled safe ground. Buy a pair that will collapse to a size small enough to fit inside your rucksack.

No other piece of winter equipment (and knowing how to use it) is more important than an ice axe. No single design performs equally well in all situations – an axe of a convenient length for walking will be awkward to climb with, and a pick set at a shallow angle for an efficient self-arrest will not perform so well when climbing.

How an axe feels is important – if it doesn't fit comfortably in your hand or the swing is not right, then there will be little incentive to use it. Ensure that the shaft is small enough for you to grip it with gloves on.

ICE AXE STANDARDS

There are two types of CE marked (European standard) ice axes:

1 **B-rated (basic) axes** Intended for hill walking and glacier walking. The shaft is strong enough to use as a belay anchor.

2 **T-rated (technical) tools** Intended for climbing and mountaineering. They are 30–40 per cent stronger to allow for more extreme use and abuse (i.e. torquing the pick into cracks).

Ice pick standards

Picks are also B- and T-rated. The latter are thicker to withstand side-to-side stresses, but they are not as good at penetrating ice. Whichever ice pick you use, it will be very difficult to break.

These axes are predominantly used as a walking stick on flat or easier-angled slopes, to arrest a fall, climb grade 1 gullies, and occasionally to cut steps.

THE SHAFT
The length of an ice axe for general purpose use has generated quite a debate over the last few years. The answer is simple; the steeper the slope, the more experienced you are and the more experienced you are on crampons, the shorter the axe can be. A length of 60–70cm is a good place to start. Longer axes are unwieldy and get in the way if the slope becomes steep, but they are the best for walking on easier-angled slopes.

WEIGHT
Light is right and B-rated is enough.

THE HEAD (PICK AND ADZE)
The head hould be a one-piece construction, with a gentle curve; too flat and it will be unstable when self-arresting and climbing; too steep and it will tend to snatch and can be wrenched out of the hand. The adze should be slightly scooped and at an angle that continues the curve from the pick. The hole in the centre of the head is for leash attachment.

THE SPIKE
A long, sharp spike is harder to hold if you need to ice axe arrest.

You should aim for a balance between performance for walking and climbing grade 3/4 climbs or winter scrambles when choosing a general mountaineering axe. It should have a natural, easy swing.

THE SHAFT
A length of 60cm is a good place to start. Gently curved models have a better swing, and the ability to plunge them into snow is not compromised. However, on easier-angled slopes (less than 60 degrees) they have no advantage.

The hand rest is a recent improvement to shaft design and improves grip and stops you banging your knuckles against the ice (it will not appreciatively affect plunging the axe into the snow). Ensure the diameter is small enough to hold with gloves on. Some ultra-light models do not have a spike, which is not a problem in hard, firm snow, but they can become blocked and they are inferior in ice.

WEIGHT AND STRENGTH
T-rated has a stronger construction overall. Light is right, but ultra-light axes are not good for penetrating hard snow. A rubber grip on the shaft will keep your hands warmer, reduce vibration and help your grip, but it can make it slightly harder to plunge the axe into hard snow.

THE HEAD
A more curved pick provides you with better hooking, but it shouldn't be so steep that it might snatch during self-arrest. The adze may be larger, but it must still follow the curve of the head to allow for easier step-cutting and digging.

Fig. 35 *The Cirque (left) and Raptor (general mountaineering axes from DMM). A dry, fresh snow ski wax makes the shaft on less technical tools stickier, giving greater grip.*

Technical axes range from those designed for all-round mixed and ice climbing, to specific steep ice and technical mixed or dry-tooling axes. Radical steep ice axes (leashed or leashless) make climbing very steep icefalls or technical mixed terrain much easier. On the average Scottish or alpine route every part of the axe is used, and features such as grip rests, triggers and strange shaft shapes can be a hindrance.

General technical tools are robust axes made for taking a lot of punishment. Use a pair from the same manufacturer, because each manufacturer's axe has a different balance and swing. One usually has a hammer (for knocking in pegs) and the other an adze. They are ideal for climbs of Grade 3+.

THE SHAFT
The shaft is usually 55cm with a bend or curve that allows easier placement on bulges and reduces knuckle bruising. On hard-mixed or waterfall climbs, a radical curve clears bulges easily, but is less balanced. It may compromise safety on alpine routes, especially on descent, and may make it more difficult to create an ice axe belay.

There are two varieties of leashless tool handles:

1 **Competition-inspired handles** With an upper and lower ergonomic grip. Most effective on very steep ground where much of one's bodyweight must be supported by the upper body (Fig. 36.4).

2 **Classically shaped axes** With a 'horn' at the base to support the hand (Fig. 36.1 and 2).

Both can often be fitted with a 'trigger finger' – a smaller 'horn', that can either be used to create a higher grip position on the axe or as additional support for one of the fingers when holding the main grip (Fig. 36.3). Well-fitting gloves are essential to maintain good contact with your tools. **Note:** Do not be tempted to climb leashless with tools that are not designed for the job.

WEIGHT AND STRENGTH

T-rated picks are heavier duty and better suited to mixed climbing. Slimmer B-rated picks penetrate ice with minimal shattering. Heavy axes penetrate better on new brittle ice.

THE HEAD

Some models have picks that can be changed before you go climbing, but only with the same manufacturer's pick. There are three main pick designs:

1 **Straight** Some climbers prefer a straighter pick for alpine work where a bit of everything can be encountered.

2 **Classic** Better balanced for general mountaineering (Fig. 35).

3 **Reverse pick** Better for hooking, ice penetration, and easier removal from steep ice. The adze is more curved and steeply drooped for hooking and torquing (Fig. 36).

Two hammers may prove more useful for pure ice climbing, but if it is your only set of tools, get an adze on one of them.

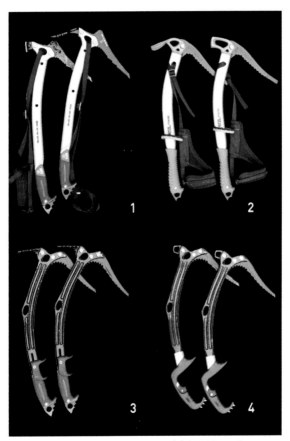

Fig. 36 *A selection of technical tools: (1) DMM Superfly (2) Petzl Aztar (3) DMM Rebel (4) DMM Anarchist*

A leash is useful for step cutting and for front pointing, but it can be a hindrance as you zigzag up or down slopes, changing your axe from hand to hand. However, if dropping your axe is a real possibility, and subsequent retrieval may be difficult, use a leash.

- Attach the leash to the axe head with a lark's foot knot, making it easy to remove.
- Do not wrap the leash around the head, because it is uncomfortable and compromises your ability to hold the axe.
- Avoid leashes that slide up and down the shaft, because they get close to your crampons when not in use.

For the majority of climbers, leashes are still important to take some of the strain off the hands, reduce the chances of dropping the axe and, should your feet lose their placement, prevent a big fall. They fall into two categories:

1 **Fixed leashes** Cheaper and lighter
2 **Clipper leashes** Allow quick and easy removal of hands from an axe, i.e. when you need to place gear or when you start to play with leashless climbing. Also allows a more ergonomic cuff design, because your hand does not have to be removed.

LENGTH
The leash must be the correct length – too long and it will not take any weight, too short and it will restrict your swing. As a rough guide, hook the wrist-supporting part of the leash on to the spike of the axe and shorten the leash until it is tight. Put your gloved hand into the wrist loop and hang from the axe; your little finger should be level with the bottom of the grip/top of the spike.

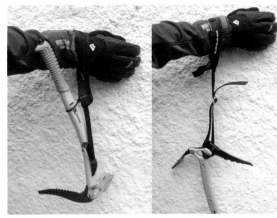

***Fig. 37** For ice climbing, the pivot point should be further along the shaft so that you can easily grab it, but for mixed climbing the axe should dangle out of the way.*

CLIMBING LEASHLESS

Leashless tools enable you to shake out more often and, with two grips on the shaft, they make it easy to transfer hands, rest and de-pump. Hands also get less cold, as the blood flow is less restricted.

However, climbing leashless is a problem when using thick mitts and iced-up grips. Leashes are also less useful on routes that require a lot of snow clearing and digging. A possible alternative to climbing leashless is to climb with a leash on one axe or to use a removable leash (opposite).

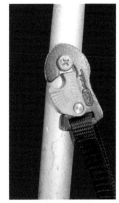

***Fig. 38** A removable leash system from Petzl*

A sharp pick saves energy when ice climbing, and also penetrates thin seams of ice and thin rock cracks on mixed ground. However, beware; a razor-sharp pick often catches on features that won't hold body weight – it is therefore better to slightly 'dampen' even the most extreme picks for mixed climbing. A moderately sharp pick is probably best for mixed climbers operating at a more normal level.

MODIFYING A PICK'S SHAPE

Unless you are climbing very high grades, keep to the manufacturer's pick shape.

- Make a master tracing on paper of the new pick.
- File it so that the tip of the pick hits the ice first until about 2cm of the pick has disappeared.
- Take a small, light, thin, metal file without a handle on big routes. A thin round 'chainsaw' file is useful for the teeth. File with the grain of the metal.
- Radical refinement of some picks improves penetration and holding power on thin ice and makes removal from ice much easier, but it may make any warranties obsolete.
- Changing the pick shape basically involves reducing the surface area of the tip of the pick. However, the thin sharp point is then easily bent and, once gone, it may not be possible to create a new point. Such picks are most useful where the pick is placed, rather than hit against, rock features.

MODIFYING THE SHAPE OF A PICK (Fig. 39)

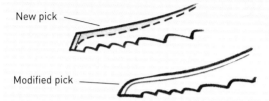

New pick

Modified pick

- Blunt the teeth close to the shaft.
- Slightly round off the sharp edges from the underside teeth and sharpen the top edge of the pick.
- Increase the angle of the first tooth so that it hooks better on thin ice and small edges.
- For mixed climbing, consider filing some teeth into the top of the pick to help with Steiner moves (p.122).

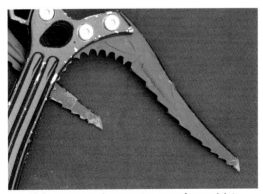

Fig. 40 *Be sure to make a master copy of your pick to match it to when you re-sharpen (DMM Rebel axe).*

USING SKI POLES

- Ski poles are not a substitute for an ice axe.
- Big baskets are better when carrying a load on flat or low-angled snow.
- When carrying an ice axe and a pole, do not put your hand through the pole's leash; you may need to discard it quickly to use your ice axe.

CRAMPONS

- Crampons are heavy and slow you down by 10–15 per cent, so when the snow conditions and terrain allow, leave them off.
- However, put crampons on before you need them, only taking them off if the walking is easier without; you won't compromise safety and you won't have to put them back on five minutes later.

Fig. 41 Leaning into the slope forces your foot off the holds – stand upright, whatever the steepness (climber C. Hebblethwaite).

KICKING STEPS

Swing from the knee and let the weight of your boot do the work – snow should fly upwards. There are two basic techniques:

1 **Slice step** The uphill edge of your boot cuts across the slope (Fig. 42)
2 **Pigeon hole step** Kick directly into the snow.

Keep steps evenly spaced and try to incline them inwards to create a platform for your foot. It is important for the followers to also kick in, and not just stand in your steps. To change direction, thrust the shaft of your axe into the snow and kick a large enough step for both feet, then change direction and continue.

DESCENDING

The slice step can be used in descent, but on steeper slopes the following methods are better.

Fig. 42 Slice steps – swing from the knee and let the weight of your boot do the work.

The plunge step (Fig. 43, p.72)

When the snow is soft, stand upright, facing outwards. Step forwards (lean down the fall line), keeping your knee straight, but not locked (the firmer the snow the straighter your leg) and plunge your heel into the snow, which forces your body weight through the straightened leg. Maintain momentum and repeat. If the snow is too solid to plunge step, you should have crampons on. Hold the axe in the cane position and plunge it into the snow, coordinating with one leg.

Fig. 43 *The plunge step forces your body weight through the straightened leg (climber C. Hebblethwaite).*

Down climb

Use this when the slope is too steep yet the snow is soft enough to do without crampons. Turn and face into the slope and kick steps, placing the axe firmly into the snow.

GLISSADING

Glissading is fast, easy to do and exhilarating, but because of this it can be highly dangerous. Control your speed, look ahead for stones, and do not attempt it when you cannot see the bottom of the slope. If you are wearing crampons, remove them or – safer still – just walk down.

Sitting glissade

This is best on soft snow. To maintain control, run the spike of the axe like a rudder along the snow to one side.

Standing glissade

Crouch with slightly bent knees and spread your arms for stability. Bring your weight from your heels to the entire foot, and off you go. Control speed by digging your heels in. Use an axe and a ski pole to the side of you to control speed, and be ready to ice axe arrest.

Make a good platform in the snow to put on your crampons, stand up, and ensure boots and crampons are clear of snow.

FLAT-FOOTING (Fig. 44)

Edging the foot into a slope only uses one row of points – it is safer and more efficient to roll your ankle and use all of the downward facing crampon points. If you find this difficult, the ankle portion of your boots may be too stiff, your ankles inflexible or you are not shifting your centre of gravity (COG) over one foot before moving the other (try undoing the top laces on your boot to make it easier).

- On lower-angled snow or ice, firmly plant all the downward facing points into the slope and walk up it with your legs slightly apart. Avoid stamping or dragging your feet.

Fig. 44 *Flat-footing uses all of the downward facing spikes on your crampons.*

Fig. 45 Walking like a duck lessens the strain on your ankles.

Fig. 46 Walking diagonally requires rhythm and balance. You must swing your leg well in front of the other one.

Ascending

- As the slope angle increases, it becomes easier to spread your feet and walk like a duck (Fig. 45).
- As the angle increases further, walk diagonally, but with your toes pointing across the slope or even downhill (Fig. 46). Eventually you will have to sidestep up the slope by planting your uphill foot firmly; push your lower foot well forward and over the upper foot to plant it solidly. Take care not to catch your crampon points or straps, or gaiters.

Descending

When descending, point your toes down the slope (Fig. 47, p.75), flex at the knees and hips, keep your feet apart and do not dig your heel in – the rear points do not work like the heel of a boot. If you cannot place all your points in, turn around and front point down.

Fig. 47 Point your toes like a Viennese horse to get all of the crampon points into the slope (climber C. Hebblethwaite).

FRONT POINTING
Only the front-facing crampon points are placed into the ice. Front pointing is the most direct way to ascend a steep slope, but the hardest on your calf muscles.

COMBINATION/AMERICAN TECHNIQUE
On moderately steep snow/ice, try to mix front pointing with flat footing.

CARRYING YOUR ICE AXE

The purpose-built carriers on your rucksack are not the best place to carry an ice axe; it is difficult to keep the sharp points away from other people and it is not easily accessible. Instead, use the compression straps down the side of your rucksack (you can even tuck the picks under the lid). On snowy or icy terrain tuck your axe down the back of your rucksack so it is to ready to hand.

Fig. 48 *Place the axe under your shoulder strap – pick upwards – and lift it over your shoulder (climber C. Hebblethwaite).*

HOLDING AN ICE AXE

Always wear gloves and keep the axe in the uphill hand. It does not matter whether you hold the pick forwards or backwards; holding it forwards makes it easier to stab quickly into hard snow should you slip, while holding it backwards makes it marginally quicker to use in self-arrest. See pp. 78–83 for a number of ways to use an ice axe effectively.

Fig. 49 *Pick forward or back? Contrary to accepted wisdom, it does not matter.*

Right twin, Aonach Mor, Scotland.

The cane or self-belay position

See Fig. 50. Hold the axe head, spike downwards. If you slip, push the axe into the snow and grasp the shaft at the surface of the snow with the other hand. If that fails, revert to the ice axe-arrest position.

Fig. 50 Self-belay should be your first line of defence if you slip (climber C. Hebblethwaite).

Cross-body position (Fig. 51)
This is a secure position when the slope is steep, especially in descent. As the angle steepens, stand upright and do not lean into the slope. Turn your body sideways to the slope, grasp the axe by the head in your downhill hand and plant the spike across your body into the slope.

Banister technique (Fig. 52)
This should be used when descending on ice. Plant the pick as far below you as possible and lift gently; the axe will lock into place. As you descend, slide your hand along the shaft to the head, then remove and repeat.

Fig. 51 *The cross-body position helps you to stand upright on steeper ground when using flat footing.*

Fig. 52 *The banister technique can provide you with extra security when descending a steep step (climber C. Hebblethwaite).*

For steeper snow or ice (45 degrees and higher) use front pointing combined with:

- **Low and high dagger** The low dagger position (Fig. 53a) is useful on moderately steep hard snow or soft ice. Face the ice and hold it by the head at the adze. Push the pick into the slope at about waist or chest level. The high dagger (Fig. 53b) is used on steeper slopes. Wrap your hand around the head of the axe with the pick facing into the slope.

- **The anchor position** Gives you more security on short sections of steep snow and/or ice. It is really front pointing using your ice axe above your head (see p.75). Hold the axe near the bottom of the shaft. Swing it to set the pick into the ice. Now, front-point your feet upwards and move both hands progressively up the axe shaft until you reach the high dagger position. Don't remove it too soon; step up into a dagger grip so that it is easier to remove. When ice is very steep, use two tools.

Fig. 53 *The low and high dagger is a comfortable way to hold the ice axe on steeper terrain (climber C. Hebblethwaite).*

CUTTING STEPS

This is useful even if you are wearing crampons on hard snow and/or ice. The most popular method is to cut 'slash steps' (a leash may help to support your hand).

- When ascending diagonally, stand in balance with the axe in your uphill hand and swing the axe from the shoulder like a pendulum until the adze makes contact with the snow.

- With successive swings, slice out a step across the fall line, inclined slightly inwards.

- To change direction, cut a large step for both feet and swap your axe to the other hand.

- When travelling horizontally, keep the steps in line, making it easier for the person following.

- In descent, hold the axe in the downhill hand, place a hand on your knee to maintain balance and slash steps.

Fig. 54 Cutting steps in descent (climber C. Hebblethwaite).

SELF-ARREST

This technique has saved lives, but on hard snow or very soft snow it is difficult to do and you should use the self belay or the pick first. Practice on a slope with a safe run-out, without crampons, but wear a helmet. Try rolling into it, sliding on your back and head-first.

Fig. 55 *Ice axe arrest*
(A) Hold the axe at 45 degrees across the chest with the adze in the crook of the shoulder. Hold the head with one hand and cover the spike with the other. To get into the break position, turn your head away from the head of the axe. Lift your feet off the snow, and lift the spike upwards to force the pick into the snow. If the axe is ripped away, relocate it in the above position and repeat.
(B) Should you fall head-first, place the pick into the snow to the side of you and then pivot around it and resume the break position.
(C) Should you fall on your back head-first, put the ice axe out at waist level and pivot around it until you are in the break position.

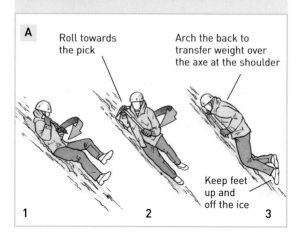

A

Roll towards the pick

Arch the back to transfer weight over the axe at the shoulder

Keep feet up and off the ice

1   2   3

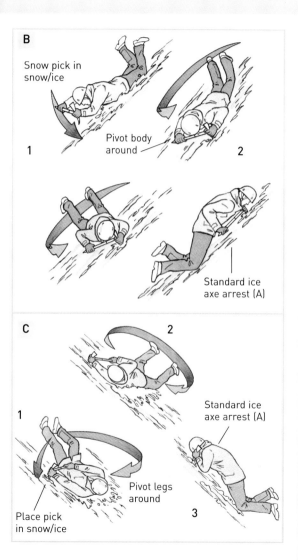

B

Snow pick in snow/ice

Pivot body around

1

2

Standard ice axe arrest (A)

C

2

Standard ice axe arrest (A)

1

Pivot legs around

Place pick in snow/ice

3

MOVING TOGETHER

Whenever you put a rope on, ask yourself what it is you are hoping to achieve. There are two reasons for putting on a rope: to stop you falling off something and to stop you falling down something. Rope-up when the climbing is easy – do not teeter on a steep slope sorting gear and putting your crampons on.

Fig. 56 *Moving together on snow is quick, but requires experience and judgement (climber C. Hebblethwaite).*

OPEN SNOW SLOPE
This is a fast method of travel, but you must both be wary of a slip. It can sometimes provide an illusion of safety and you may be safer running the rope out to a quick snow belay or even soloing. The rope should be short (1.5–2m) and kept tight between climbers with no hand coils (Fig. 56). See methods for shortening the rope in *Rucksack Guide: Alpinism* (A&C Black, 2009).

HORIZONTAL SNOW CRESTS
You should be 5–10m apart (with the strongest climber at the back) with 1 or 2m of coils in each climber's hand, which can be dropped should a climber slip

(shout, because the other climber may be looking at their feet). The other climber must then step or jump down to the opposite side, to counterbalance the fallen climber. If there are spikes of rock and boulders along the ridge, drop the hand coils and weave in and out using the natural features as running belays.

Fig. 57 *On horizontal snow crests carry hand coils to give yourself time to react should someone fall off.*

STEEP MIXED RIDGES
You should be at least 5–15m apart with the rope clipped into runners.

SHORT MIXED STEPS
Spotting is difficult and dangerous, because of the number of spikes that will fly towards you. Use the rope and direct belays whenever possible to minimise delays.

LONGER STEPS
Use techniques akin to rock climbing where the leader is belayed and the belayer anchored; again, direct belaying will speed things up.

MOVING TOGETHER

Fig. 58 *On exposed mixed ridges place protection – you never know when you may slip (climber C. Hebblethwaite).*

SHORT ROPING ON DESCENT

This technique requires constant vigilance and only protects the lower climber. Without considerable practice it can compromise the safety of the team. It may be safer to solo, and then at least only one of you falls. The distance between climbers should be as short as possible.

Fig. 59 *Short roping requires constant vigilance to do it well (climbers C. Hebblethwaite and S. Ponsford).*

A good winter climber prepares their gear, looks after their hands and feet and retreats when conditions are bad.

Rope work techniques are largely the same as those used in summer rock climbing, but you are wearing gloves and have snow pouring down your neck!

The best ice climbing protection is rock climbing gear, because it is more reliable and quicker to place. However, many ice routes require at least eight screws; three for a belay, two as runners and three for the next belay.

A dedicated winter rack may be preferable, because gear is often damaged when hammered into icy cracks. Some climbers drill holes into old-style hexes to reduce the weight. Thread them with 5.5mm Dyneema cord, so that the knot can be tied inside the hex, reducing the likelihood of damage.

Cams are of limited use in icy cracks (tri cams work better), but carry a few. Pegs are essential when nuts will not fit (thread them with short loops of 4mm cord for easier racking). When you carry two sets of wires rack them separately in full sets – if you drop a set, you still have the full range. Spray-paint your gear in different colours for easy identification.

EXPERT TIP

Clive Hebblethwaite MIC
clive.hebblethwaite@ntlworld.com

'It's a myth that belays in winter are always poor. It's just that it takes more persistence to say, "No, that won't do," and to clear some more snow or ice. Save time by looking generally in a few places first before deciding which place to focus your efforts, but don't over focus!'

SHOCK SLINGS

Shock slings reduce the impact force (IF) by rupturing the stitching in a controlled manner. They may be useful on marginal gear, such as ice screws, but their usefulness is limited to short falls (5m) and a fall factor (FF) of 0.5. An equivalent amount of energy is reduced if you reverse 1m before falling off or the belayer pays out a little rope as you fall (see forces and falling in *Rucksack Guide: Rock Climbing*, A&C Black, 2009).

FINDING PROTECTION IN MIXED GROUND

Experience will tell you when it is worth spending time clearing snow and when it is better to climb on.

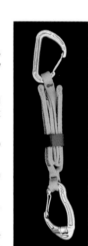

- Never pass good runners; you may never know where the next one will be.

- Use 60m ropes to allow you to go that bit further.

- Look for signs – has anyone been digging there before?

- Look for old pegs, cracks, shattered rock, etc.

- Dig for proper cracks and move on rather than persevere with blind corners.

- Use ice screws to help prevent rock protection lifting out if it is poor.

Fig. 60 DMM *Ripstop sling*

ICE SCREW CARRIERS

Several firms produce specialist ice screw racks. Look for one that is easy to use while wearing gloves and which keeps bulk to a minimum.

ROPES

Ropes should be dry treated 50m, 60m or even 70m lengths on some long ice pitches. Most climbers use double or half ropes for winter climbing, because the routes often wander, the impact force is reduced and abseiling is easier. However, on direct ice routes a single rope with a thinner abseil line dragged behind the second is useful, because it is lighter and there is little drag.

CARRYING PROTECTION

If you are not wearing a rucksack, a bandolier or a lightweight chest harness is better, but on steeper climbs gear can then hang behind you and be difficult to reach.

- Rack ice screws higher on the chest for ice-fall climbing so you can see them.
- When you are wearing a rucksack, hang gear from the shoulder straps or dedicated gear racks on the shoulder straps or waist belt. You can make your own with 6mm cord and clear plastic tubing – experiment with the best place to hang it from your particular rucksack.

A snow anchor's strength depends on the consistency of the snow and the surface area of the object buried; in powder snow nothing will hold. Some of the anchors described here are too time-consuming to be used as runners during a climb and are likely only to be used for creating a belay.

BURIED AXE (Figs 61 and 71)
Radically curved ice axes may compromise the holding power in uncertain snow conditions.

- Dig a clean slot using the adze in undisturbed snow, perpendicular to the direction of loading; the front, load wall of the slot should incline slightly to prevent the axe lifting.

- Next, cut a narrow slot using the spike, just big enough for a sling to fit into and the same depth as the ice axe slot, which will prevent the axe being lifted out.

- Attach a sling with a clove hitch or lark's foot at a point on the axe that ensures the surface area is the same on both sides of the sling. Do not use the balance point, as it invariably pulls through at the head end.

- Firmly place the axe, pick downwards, into the snow.

- Driving another axe or ski pole, just back from vertical, through the sling in front of the horizontal axe reinforces the anchor (see Fig. 62).

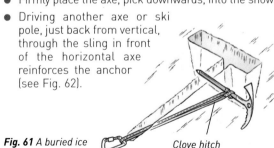

Fig. 61 *A buried ice axe belay*

Clove hitch

SNOW STAKES

Snow stakes can be placed upright in very firm snow or buried like an axe when the snow is softer.

- If you can push it in by hand it is unlikely to be secure.
- A T-shaped profile may have better holding power in softer snow than a buried axe belay.
- On steep slopes, stakes should be placed at approximately 45 degrees from the direction of pull; on gentler slopes the angle can be less.

Fig. 62 A buried axe anchor

DEADMAN OR SNOW FLUKE

A deadman is a specially shaped, aluminium plate with a metal cable attached. It is useful as a belay anchor and as a runner, and is most useful in slush or moist and heavy snow. It is best placed at about 40 degrees from the direction of pull, with a deep slot to allow the cable to run directly to the belayer. However, great care must be taken to ensure that you dig deep enough and that there are no hard layers to deflect the deadman.

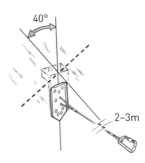

Fig. 63 The correct placement of a deadman

SNOW BOLLARD

- The bollard should be horseshoe-shaped, and not tear-dropped, to keep as much snow in the anchor as possible.

- The bollard can be padded with cardboard, clothing or ice axes to stop the rope cutting through the snow.

- If it is used as an abseil anchor, the ice axes and padding can be removed when the last person abseils.

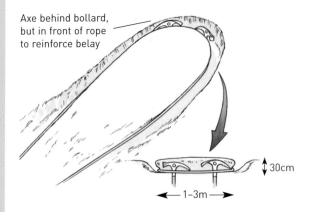

Axe behind bollard, but in front of rope to reinforce belay

30cm

1–3m

Fig. 64 Snow bollards are strong and reliable in good snow.

NATURAL ANCHORS

On waterfall ice, thread sturdy ice columns with a sling. Use cracks between the ice and rock by clove hitching an ice screw with Dyneema cord (the threads can cut a tape sling) and placing it in the crack at 90 degrees to create a chockstone.

ICE HOOKS

Ice hooks, e.g. DMM Bulldog, fit in places where nuts and pegs will not: they can be placed in rock cracks, turf, between ice features such as icicles or into old tool placement holes, but

Fig. 65 Never pass good runners; you may never know where the next one will be (the author climbing, Scotland).

their holding power is always questionable. Often this hook can be hand placed, or simply tapped to seat. A stubby screw in thin ice or an angle peg in an ice choked crack will, however, be stronger. Some ice climbers advocate using them on free hanging ice pillars, because they may come out if the pillar collapses.

For mixed climbing, the standard ice hook is too long, so you will have to modify an existing design.

Fig. 66 A DMM Bulldog ice hook

Some climbers recommend shortening the hook by half and reshaping the pick to resemble your ice axe pick. If it matches the shape, and if your pick finds a tight spot, you can place your hook once it's removed.

WARHOGS OR ICE PEGS

Pound-in protection is useful in frozen turf or mud, and commonly used on Scottish routes.

ICE SCREWS

Tests by Black Diamond have shown that an ice screw placed at a positive angle will hold better (Fig. 67). The theory is that the surface area of screw threads is greater than the tube length and provides better holding power. This is fine for perfect ice, but we rarely experience perfect ice. Placing all ice screws at a positive angle could lead to failure in some situations, especially if the ice is detached, hollow, slushy or rotten. It may be better in many instances to rely on the lever resistance (negative angle) of the screw, rather than the holding power of the threads.

CHEAP ICE SCREWS

Don't waste your money on cheap ice screws and forget 'drive-in' ice pegs for pure ice.

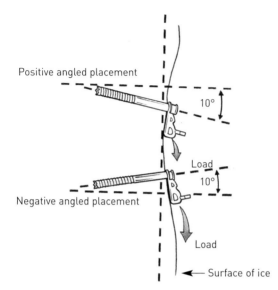

Fig. 67 *Angle of ice screw placement*

- The quality of the ice is more important than screw length or screw diameter, but a fully inserted (into the hanger), large diameter screw is stronger than a small diameter screw of the same length, and the longer the screw, the better it will hold.

- When you are close to the ground, or belay, you have the potential to generate a greater impact force (IF) on your protection, so the placements should be as strong as possible.

- Place ripper slings on the first two ice screws of a pitch and whenever you doubt a placement.

- Use longer screws when close to the belay or even equalise two placements when the quality of the ice is questionable.

SNOW AND ICE ANCHORS

Assessing the quality of ice

Ice is at its best between 0 and –5°C. Above this temperature, surface thawing reduces the holding power of screws considerably. Colder temperatures may make the ice far more brittle and fragile.

- **Dense ice** is generally clear (glassy), bluer and contains less air – use a positive angled screw.
- **Less dense ice** is greyish, opaque and often has bubbles – use a negative angled screw.
- Look for dense, shaded ice behind pillars and other features.
- Clear away poor quality ice to get to the better stuff underneath.
- Only place ice screws into large, solid free-hanging pillars; if they collapse you do not want to be attached.
- Be careful when using old ice screw holes, as they may be too large.

Brittleness, plating and layering as you climb

Low-density ice often receives picks without creating much surface deformation, but high-density ice must be displaced as the pick enters, revealing a pit or cracking.

As you turn the screw there should be even resistance to turning. If you don't need to use the handle, it may be better to place it at zero or negative angle. If you feel the screw break through into less dense layers, remove it and place it at a negative angle.

Tying off ice screws

If the screw sticks out less than 5cm, just clip the eye or use a wired runner on the screw. There are now some very short ice screws to avoid having to tie them off.

Looking after ice screws

After climbing, dry your screws (inside as well as out) and, using an undamaged screw as a guide, touch up any damage to the teeth with a small round metal file. For advice on sharpening ice screws go to www.blackdiamondequipment.com.

ABALAKOV V-THREAD

In good ice, the Abalakov V-thread (Fig. 68) is useful for belay or abseil stations or top rope set-ups. Do not trust old Abalakovs, and test them while still on the abseil or belay rope. You will need two 22cm ice screws, a length of 7mm cord and a wire coat hanger with a hook or purpose-made puller.

- Insert the ice screws at a 10-degree angle uphill to the slope, and a 60-degree angle sideways.

- Make tunnels with the two screws in the middle.

- The greater the distance between the two tubes, the stronger the thread.

- Leave the first screw in place as a marker for the second tube.

- Thread cord through the tunnel and use the puller to retrieve it. If you haven't got a wire, enlarge the hole and capture the cord by twisting an ice screw.

- Move the cord back and forth to smooth out the tunnel and tie a knot to create your anchor (tie a triple fisherman's knot in Dyneema cord).

Fig. 68 The Abalakov V-thread anchor

CLIMBING ON SNOW

When a rock or ice screw belay cannot be found, an indirect belay method such as a buried axe (Fig. 70), snow stake or deadman is best (pp. 92–3. A snow bollard is too time-consuming and is used mainly for abseiling). The anchors can be doubled up if the snow is poor, but do not disturb the snow of one anchor when placing the other.

***Fig. 69** When rock anchors are not available use a waist belay.*

- After creating your anchor, cut out a deep bucket seat 2m below the axe, with slots for your legs (at least as deep as your thighs) and a ledge for the rope to lie on (Fig. 70, opposite).

- Sit on a pad and waist belay, because it is the most dynamic system. Clip a krab to the front of your harness and to the leader's rope to prevent the belay being ripped from your body should you fall.

- When your belay is beyond doubt it is possible to use a belay tube. If in doubt, keep to a waist belay.

- In all belay methods, it is vital to place a runner as soon as you leave the stance to prevent a fall factor two (FF2) on to the belay.

Clove hitch

To climber

Brake hand

Fig. 70 Creating a belay on snow using a buried axe with a bucket seat. The climber's rope is on the same side as the rope to the axe.

STOMPER BELAY

This is a quick and easy method for belaying a second climber in non-serious terrain, especially when the snow is poor. However, it has serious limitations – should the second fall and end up on steep or overhanging ground, you can do nothing to help, and escape from the system is impossible. The forces generated in a fall pull the belayer down into the axe, increasing its holding power. Use a shoulder belay with the krab slotted on to the shaft of the axe (do not put an Italian hitch on to the krab, as it will redirect the forces to the axe).

Fig. 71 The stomper belay – a quick belay method, but only use it when the climber won't end up dangling in space (climber C. Hebblethwaite).

SCOTTISH BELAY

This is not as reliable as the stomper, and should only be used when the snow is firm. It has the advantage that you can escape from the system more easily. Plant the axe and lark's foot a short sling with a krab to the shaft. Take the rope through the krab and waist belay. A krab linking your harness to the live rope will stop it being pulled from your waist during a fall.

Fig. 72 The Scottish belay (climber C. Hebblethwaite)

CLIMBING ON SNOW

BOOT AXE BELAY

This is a rapid method, but it is bad for your back. Like the methods on pp. 100–1 it is only suitable for bringing a second up the pitch. It should not be used for protecting someone in serious terrain, e.g. when crossing a crevasse.

Fig. 73 A boot axe belay – do not use it to protect someone in serious terrain.

Top of a Cairngorm gully,
Scotland (climber Dodi Jepson)

Ask yourself the following questions:

- Are other climbers on your route and is it safe to climb behind them?
- What are the prevailing conditions – is it too warm (which means there is a risk of collapse) or is it too cold (sudden big drops in temperature can make ice falls extremely fragile and prone to collapse)?
- Have you broken the route into manageable sections, like you would when rock climbing?
- Have you found places where the white/grey ice gives way to the better plastic, blue ice?
- Where are the rest places?
- Can you bridge or get close to the rock to place a runner?

Place yourself and your belayer away from falling ice, rack up slowly and methodically with a calm mind and put on your harness before your crampons. Whether to anchor the belayer to the ground will depend on the consequences of a fall (see *Rucksack Guide: Rock Climbing*, A&C Black, 2009).

CONSIDERATIONS FOR BOTTOM ROPING ICE CLIMBS
Beware that when you use ice screws as anchors and leave them in place for a long time they may melt out, due to heat generated by the pressure. Use three equalised screws and cover them with snow/ice to protect them from the Sun.

A steep ice route requires a cool head (Devil's Appendix, North Wales).

STEEP ICE CLIMBING

Before swinging, touch the ice with your pick at the point you want to hit. Practice swinging at a marked spot and watch the pick all the way. Do not stretch up too far, because it is then hard to get the axe out from a poor placement.

Fig. 74 *Swinging an ice axe is akin to swinging a badminton racket. Keep your shoulder, wrist and axe in line.*

MISTAKES WHEN PLACING YOUR ICE AXES

- Elbows too low
- Not relaxing the wrist
- Taking your eye off the spot
- Gripping the axe too hard, preventing the natural rotation of the hand
- Putting your arm out to the side and not keeping it in line with the axe.

Your swing should be relaxed, using the weight of the axe head to do the work and not your shoulder or body. Your aim is to penetrate the ice enough, but not too much.

- Prepare the swing by dropping the axe head behind your shoulder, far enough to hit your rucksack (if you are wearing one), and relax your wrist (Fig. 74, opposite).
- Start the swing with the shoulder and progressively straighten the arm, keeping your shoulder, wrist and axe in a straight line.
- At the moment of impact, snap the wrist forward to increase the strike force, and release the hand to maintain the kinetic energy of the axe head and to keep blood flowing (it also stops your fist punching the ice).
- Your arm should be slightly bent when the pick hits the ice (the position of maximum power).
- A good placement makes a 'thunk' sound.
- If the ice 'dinner plates', there may be better quality ice underneath, so clear the shattered ice away.

To improve your placements and efficiency:

- Look for depressions in the ice where the ice is more dense than on bulges and will resist fracturing.
- Hook the pick into the holes left by other climbers; if it does not feel good, gently tap it with your other axe.
- Hook between icicles where the ice is often compressed and more solid.
- On good quality ice a single sure swing is best.
- On brittle or thin ice little short swings/taps from the wrist and not the shoulder are better.
- Think ahead: cut stances for your feet, to give your calf muscles a rest.
- If you have to remove ice do it carefully, and take icicles off bit by bit.

REMOVING A STUCK TOOL

Lift the tool out the way it went in. If it is stuck, push up on the adze or hammer to lift it out. Do not wiggle the pick from side to side, as this can weaken it.

Fig. 75 *Push upwards on the adze or hammer to remove a stuck tool.*

PLACING YOUR FEET

- Take many small steps and swing from the knee, and not the whole leg, letting the weight of your boot do the work.

- Kicking too hard simply makes the boot bounce off the ice. If the ice is hard, kick twice: once to shatter the ice and the second to get to the good ice underneath.

- Kick perpendicular to the ice so that both front points go in. Once the front points have engaged, drop your heel so that the secondary front points make contact.

- Standing on your toes raises your heels, forcing the front points down, possibly causing them to sheer.
- The shape of the ice may force you to kick out to the side. To do this turn your whole boot to get the front and secondary points in contact with the ice.
- Look for natural ledges where the foot can be placed sideways, relieving strain on the calves.

Fig. 76 Swing from the knee, and not the whole leg, unless you are climbing over a bulge.

Fig. 77 Do not stand on tiptoes as it forces the front points out of the ice and the secondary points to disengage (B). Keeping your heels down engages the secondary points and relaxes your calf muscles (A).

STEEP ICE CLIMBING

Before leading on an ice route, ensure that you:

- are fluid in axe and feet placement;
- can shift your centre of gravity around using your hips;
- understand the importance of keeping your hips into the wall when placing your axe and freeing them to move your feet.

The old fashioned technique of planting two axes above your head at the same height to create an X with your body is a slow method of climbing and can feel insecure, as your body will want to twist towards one of the axes when you remove the other (Fig. 78). It is, however, still a reasonable technique for moderately angled ice.

Fig. 78 Placing your ice axes and legs in an X configuration on steep ice means that when you remove one of your axes you are likely to pivot off.

TRIANGLE TECHNIQUE

For steeper ice, the triangle position sequence is better, because it allows you to adopt a balanced rest position on your legs with only one axe placed. At first, the triangle technique can seem more difficult and tiring, because you are only pulling on one tool instead

of two. However, it uses half the number of swings. Additionally, having the tools placed at different heights reduces the chances of the ice 'dinner plating'.

Fig. 79 *The triangle position sequence*
- *Start in the triangle position (A) with your crampons at the same height, your knees slightly bent and your legs slightly apart. One axe should be above your head along an imaginary line that runs through your head, hips and between your feet to form a triangle. Your hips should be pushed towards the ice and your chest and shoulders away from the ice.*
- *Now, lower your hips and hang your chest from the highest arm (B) then make three short steps. The first foot moved should be the one furthest from the lower axe. The first step should be short, and then bigger steps can be taken (C). To lift a leg, shift your hips over the weight-supporting foot. These continuous hip movements to the right and left as you move your feet (the same as transferring your COG in rock climbing) are the secret to moving smoothly (D). Move each foot up to mid-shin level then straighten the legs until you are in a new triangle position (E). The higher you take your feet the further you must move your hips.*
- *From this position, look up for your next tool place-ment; remove the lower tool and place it about a foot higher than the other tool and no more than a shoulder width away from it (F, G). Take two steps up and sideways to return to the triangle position (H, I, J, K).*

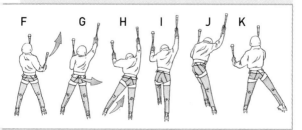

Even vertical ice feels as if it is overhanging, because your axes force you out from the ice. As the ice steepens and the surface becomes irregular with bulges and pillars, the more you have to move away from the basic triangle and engage the movement skills of rock climbing.

As you progress you may find it sometimes difficult to get back into a triangle position. When this occurs, use the left/right rule, flagging and frogging (Figs 79 and 80) adopted from rock climbing to stay in balance, e.g. right axe high and your left leg under the axe. The other foot can be splayed to the side like an outrigger (Fig. 80). Once you have mastered the basic triangle progression, try bridging between pillars and bulges and even the rock out to the side. Use back steps, heel hooks (with a spike on the back of your crampon), side-pulls and underclings.

Fig. 80 Flagging the leg when you cannot get into the triangle position.

On more difficult ice climbs you will come across icicles; cauliflower, mushroom and fragile ice; and air pockets. It may be better to hook or wedge these, so that swinging the axe does not destroy them.

On thin or fragile ice, it may be difficult to place or hook both tools. Try to hook one pick on the head of the other so that you can use the strength of both arms to obtain a higher placement. Practice searching for rest positions, however unortho-dox, and that terrifying pitch will start to look like a reasonable proposition.

Fig. 81 Frogging

This should be performed using the same method as mantleshelfing in rock climbing, but often climbers stretch too far over the bulge and cannot see or use their feet.

- Place an axe just below the bulge and walk your feet up. Release the lower tool and place it over the bulge at a comfortable distance (bent shafts make this easier) to still allow you to keep your hips away from the ice.

- Kicking in the conventional manner (where your knee joint acts as a hinge) leaves your front points downwards as they penetrate, and usually you must drop your heel to engage the secondary point.

- To go over a bulge gently, lock your leg and swing from the hip. This keeps your toes higher than your heels, helping to engage your front and secondary points at the moment of impact.

- Hang straight-armed from the higher tool and bring your feet up in small steps until you are over the bulge.

- Slide your hands along the shaft until you are almost standing, then remove the axe.

COMMON ERRORS WHEN ICE CLIMBING
- Arms are too bent
- Chest is not far enough away from the wall
- Legs are not the same height
- Gripping the tool too tightly
- Ice axes are the same height.

This is described for moving right. Practice this method by traversing back and forth at ground level.

- Start in the triangle position (A).
- Place your axe 0.75m out to the side and move your weight over the right leg (B). The other leg may end up in a counterbalance position.
- The foot used for counterbalance then crosses in front or behind of the weighted leg and is placed using the front points (C).
- The second step allows one to come back to the triangle position under the new placement (D). It is also possible to shuffle your feet along the wall.
- Continue the traverse by crossing one tool over the other (E). You will have to rotate your chest to do this, and remember to pull on the axe in the direction it is placed, and not straight down.
- Ensure that you are in a triangle position when removing a tool otherwise you will spin off the existing tool. You can use the holes made by the previous placements.

A   **B**   **C**   **D**   **E**

Fig. 82 *The sequence of movements for traversing*

PLACING ICE SCREWS

You should try to place ice screws at hip level, which will allow you to use your hips to push. You will also fall a shorter distance than if you were reaching above your head.

Place a tool solidly and, from the basic triangle position, remove your hand or leash from the lower axe and place a screw at stomach height. On steep ice it is less tiring to chop a small ledge on which to rest your crampons.

REMOVING ICE SCREWS

Clean the ice out immediately by tapping the hanger (not the threads) facing downwards (most screws are tapered

Fig. 83 Push from your hips when starting an ice screw (S. Ponsford).

internally) against the ice. Do not poke them with an ice axe – internal scratches will increase the chances of the ice sticking in the future. If this fails, start another placement to dislodge the ice or place them some-where warm until it falls out, e.g. inside your jacket.

TROUBLESHOOTING PLACING AN ICE SCREW

- Your legs are not at the same height and your COG is off centre.
- Your higher arm is not in a triangle position.
- Your hips are not pushed into the wall with the result that you must pull on your axes.
- Your chest is too close to the ice.
- Your axes are at the same height.
- You are placing the screw too high.

Think about the position of the belay for the next pitch – is the second going to be bombarded with ice? The perfect ice belay has at least two screws placed 10–15cm apart and 30–50cm one above the other. Use slings to equalise the anchors to a single point and attach your rope to it. To improve the dynamic element, place a ripper sling between you and the belay. Do not worry about upward pulls; focus on preventing a fall factor two (FF2) on to the belay. The leader should place an ice screw with a ripper sling on it immediately upon leaving the belay to prevent an FF2. It is also possible for the belay to have an extra ice screw, which the second's rope passes when belaying – this can then serve as the first screw on the next pitch.

With cold hands, mitts, icy ropes and minimal rope drag, your belaying technique must be good. If the belay is good, then belay the second directly from the anchors using a Petzl Reverso or a Plaquette, but change to belaying from your waist if they are leading. Take care when bringing two climbers up a route at the same time, because the lower one will be bombarded by ice from the first climber.

Fig. 84 *Always think of FF2 when creating an ice belay (climbers S. Ponsford and C. Trull).*

The pioneers of Scottish winter climbing did not have leashes on their axes and could climb only steep snow and chimney, gully and ridge routes. With the advent of front points and drooped picks, leashes appeared, allowing the steep ice routes and hoar-frosted buttresses to be tackled. Approximately ten years ago, competition ice climbers started the 'leashless' revolution and the circle of reinvention continued.

Early dry tooling routes followed dry rock to reach free hanging icicles, but the sport has developed so much that climbs are now being developed on rock devoid of snow or ice. It seems that this progression in the sport closely resembles the radical, challenging development of sport climbing. When such changes are afoot, the boundaries of different sub-disciplines become challenged and developed. Modern practitioners feel that bolt-protected mixed climbing could contribute much to the rich heritage of traditionally protected, ground-up and on-site mixed climbing. Signs of this are already evident in all the major mixed venues around the world, and not least in the big mountains.

TIPS FOR BETTER MIXED CLIMBING

- File the bottom of the pick to an aggressive point for supreme 'hookability'.
- Tape your leashes one-third of the way down the ice axe shaft for reduced leverage.
- Try grabbing the axe low enough below the head to resist levering off on the placement.
- A sticky glove, a rubberised shaft or surf wax will maximise grip.

MIXED CLIMBING EQUIPMENT

For mixed climbing, get modular tools with sturdy, drooped picks. Choose leashes with wide comfortable wrist loops that lock tight. Crampons should be the step-in variety with replaceable front points. On mixed ground, mono points do what slippers did for sport climbing – they add precision. For climbing in less than Arctic conditions, leather boots – especially those with insulation – are best.

EXPERT TIP

Matt Spencely – Competition mixed climber and explorer
www.greenlandexpeditions.com

'When pushing the boat out on mixed climbing where there's little snow about, skateboard grip tape wrapped around your axes offers a lot of purchase for your hands. On snowy ground, avoid grip tape like the plague!'

Fig. 85 *Using a stein pull. Mixed routes are more difficult with leashed tools. Leashless mixed climbing is faster, more creative and less painful on the wrists (climber C. Hebblethwaite).*

When there is only a dusting of white on the cliffs, the difference between techniques for dry tooling and traditional mixed climbing becomes blurred.

Full on M climbers use two hammers (or none at all), but for more traditional mixed climbing keep your adze (a beefy model) handy for the odd soft snow and turf section.

Mixed climbing uses the full gambit of rock, ice and even aid climbing skills, but with an axe and crampons – from heel hooks, drop-knees (Egyptians) and lay-backing, to a huge range of often devious tricks to win vertical height, such as figure-4s, -8s and -9s, that are beyond the scope of this book.

Look out for features to climb – there is an art to 'feeling' just how good a potential hold is from below with your picks. Move up on a previously un-tested hold with some trepidation, and keep your axe as still as possible, while keeping your face out of line should it break free.

Fig. 86 Climbing snowed-up rock requires the use of a mixture of dry tooling and mixed climbing techniques.

Ice tools can be used in a variety of ways for hooking on edges, flakes and chockstones. Bring your rock climbing skills into play, use side-pulls and under-clings and remember the axe also has an adze.

Mixed climbing often means that snow must be cleared away to reveal the natural features of the rock. However, you can also drag your axe through the snow until you feel it hook on something beneath the surface. A test pull from the shoulder will tell whether it is a placement that will hold.

Climb with your arms as straight as possible – this will require good hip and shoulder rotation. Keep your axe still and keep the shaft close to the rock to maintain a proper downward force as you try to gain height. This will require body tension between your feet and the pick. It is a difficult concept for a rock climber who is able to adjust the degree of grip.

Experiment with holding your axe further up the shaft or on the upper handle (with leashless tools) to gain extra reach towards the next placement. Such a move will change the pick balance and can send you flying. If the hold is questionable, try to move around on the axe as little as possible. Experiment (in a safe position) with a little outward pull on the axe to find out what will hold. It is also possible to hook sideways/parallel on an edge.

THE STEIN PULL

The 'stein pull' (Figs 85 and 87), named after pulling a stein of beer, is where the pick and the head of your axe are working in opposition. They can be found under overlaps, but any three-dimensional feature in the rock works, as long as there is something for the top of the tool to brace against.

Stein pulls are very stable, because the tool is firmly wedged and you can reach further, pulling out as well as down. Be sure the hold is solid enough to withstand the leverage forces involved.

Stein pulls are abundant on roofs, because the pick often slots into cracks or holes, orientating the shaft parallel to the ground like a chin-up bar.

Inverted stein pulls (Fig. 85) are achieved by reversing your grip on the tool, thumb towards the adze or hammer. Pulling down on the grip then cams the head firmly against the wall, creating a stable position.

Using stein pulls to rest

If you're climbing leashless, stein pulls can create a variety of no-hands rests. The most basic stein pull rest is the arm hook, but the leg hook is equally effective. Modern ethics on the hardest routes make any use of axes for anything other than the hands a no-go area; however for mere mortals it is fine!

Fig. 87 *A stein pull*

The technique you use will depend on the amount of ice that you are confronted with.

● When the ice is thin, use controlled, gentle blows and place your thumb against the back of the tool's grip to stabilise and direct your swing.

● If the ice is super-thin, gently chip a hookable divot, instead of planting the pick.

● In soft or chossy rock, thin or closed cracks devoid of ice can be dry tooled.

● When the ice is thicker, swing hard and on target to sink the pick into the crack like a peg. If you're feeling brave you can tap the pick in further by hammering it with your other tool!

Fig. 88 *Stacking axes when the holds are limited can help you to gain height.*

Fig. 89 *Use the hammer and adze instead of the picks (climber C. Hebblethwaite).*

Flakes and chockstones can be simply hooked by the pick or adze of your axe, but cracks without ice often require the art of torquing – jamming any part of your axe, including the hammer or the shaft, into a crack and levering it to stay in position. This can be practiced on old quarries and brick walls. Focus on keeping the pressure on the torque.

When there is only one good placement, you can stack your axes. Hook the pick of the good placement with the other tool, gain height and then place your free axe.

Fig. 90 *Matt Spencely dry-tooling in Europe*

Be wary of old guidebooks, old timers and unrepeated routes – the grading system was completely over-hauled in the early 1990s.

SCOTLAND

GRADE	DESCRIPTION
Grade I	Snow gullies (no more than 45 degrees) or easy ridges, that can sometimes have scant protection, and cornices can cause a problem. They are often used as descents and can usually be climbed with a single axe.
Grade II	Steeper with short icy or technical sections. Ridges are easy scrambles in summer. It is likely that two axes will be essential.
Grade III	Sustained ridges, or gullies, with short but steep ice (60–70 degrees), or easier buttresses and snowed-up rock routes.
Grade IV	The start of real technical difficulties. Snowed-up rock routes will be sustained, and sometimes steep and more advanced techniques will be required. Ice routes will be 70–5 degrees or have short vertical steps.
Grade V	Sustained steep ice at 70–5 degrees. Mixed routes could be up to VS (very severe) summer routes and may require the linking of multiple advanced moves.
Grade VI	Long vertical sections of ice, with little chance of rest. Mixed routes will be as for Grade V, but harder and more sustained. Mixed routes will be at least VS (very severe) summer routes.
Grade VII	Ice climbs are very serious with poorly protected steep ice. Snowed-up rock routes could have overhanging sections, even roofs.

Grade VIII   Only two ice climbs reach these heights, both are in Torridon, west coast of Scotland, and both are potential chop routes. Snowed-up rock routes follow the lines of E1s and 2s.

Grade IX   The realms of the modern elite

TECHNICAL GRADE

This refers to the technical difficulties of the pitch and takes into account the angle of the icefall, whether the climbing is sustained or not, the nature of the fall's formation, and the nature of its protection.

GRADE	DESCRIPTION
1	Easy angled ice that has no particularly hard sections
2	Easily protected pitch on good ice
3	Some 80° sections, but on thick, compact ice, with comfortable, well-protected belays
4	Sustained and near-vertical pitch, or a short pitch with a short, vertical section. Good ice and satisfactory gear.
5	Sustained and nearly always-vertical pitch up discreet ice, or a less sustained pitch that is technically more demanding. Few rests.
6	Very sustained pitch that offers no rests at all. Difficult ice; some overlaps and other formations requiring good technique. Protection is difficult to place and often of dubious nature.
7	Very sustained pitch that offers no rests at all. Is extremely fragile and technically difficult ice. Protection is run-out or non-existent.

WATER ICE AND ALPINE ICE GRADES

Ice climbing ratings are highly variable by region and are still evolving. The WI acronym implies seasonal ice; AI is often substituted for year-round alpine ice and may be easier than a WI grade with the same number.

GRADE	DESCRIPTIONS
WI 1	Low angle ice; ice axe required. General angle: 50 degrees.
WI 2	Consistent 60-degree ice with possible bulges; good protection and anchors.
WI 3	Sustained 70 degrees with possible long bulges of 80–90 degrees; reasonable rests and good stances for placing screws. Generally good protection, and screws can be placed from comfortable stances. The ice is usually of good quality.
WI 4	Sustained climbing with some vertical sections, separated by good belays. The ice may have some technical features like chandeliers, but generally the quality of ice is good and offers secure protection and belays. General angle: 80 degrees.
WI 5	A long, steep, strenuous, columnar pitch of ice. Sustained with little opportunity to rest. Expertise in dealing with the different ice formations is required (e.g. chandeliers, cauliflowers, candled sections). Adequate protection, but requires effort to place. The climb may sometimes be run-out above protection. Belays may be difficult to create or hang. General angle: 90 degrees.

WI 6   A serious lead on severe or thin ice. Long vertical or overhanging sections, which leads to extremely sustained difficulties. There are few, if any, resting sites. Ice may not be of the best quality; often thin, chandeliered and hard to protect. Hanging belays of dubious quality may be required. General angle: 90+ degrees.

WI 7   Ice is very thin, long, overhanging or very technical. There are free-hanging columns of dubious adhesion. Protection may be non-existent. The pitch is very physical and emotional. Belays require a very high level of expertise, and may be marginal. This grade applies to only a handful of routes led by an even fewer number of world-class climbers. General angle: 90++ degrees.

MIXED ROUTE/DRY TOOLING GRADES

Scottish winter climbs encompass traditional mixed climbing within the grading system, but modern mixed climbing uses Jeff Lowe's M grade. This generally focuses on routes with gymnastic dificulty and good pre-placed protection. 'M' indicates that the route is mixed, e.g. rock and ice, and the number indicates the technical difficulty.

GRADE	DESCRIPTION
M1–3	Easy. Low-angle and usually no tools.
M4	Slabby to vertical with some technical dry tooling
M5	Some sustained vertical dry tooling
M6	Vertical to overhanging with difficult dry tooling
M7	Overhanging; powerful and technical dry tooling; less than 10m of hard climbing
M8	Some nearly horizontal overhangs requiring very powerful and technical dry tooling; bouldery or longer cruxes than M7
M9	Either continuously vertical or slightly overhanging with marginal or technical holds, or a juggy roof of two to three body lengths
M10	At least 10m of horizontal rock or 30m of overhanging dry tooling with powerful moves and no rests
M11	A rope length of overhanging gymnastic climbing, or up to 15m (49ft) of roof
M12	M11 with bouldery, dynamic moves and tenuous technical holds

NORTH AMERICAN AVALANCHE DANGER SCALE

The following scale is used in the United States and Canada.

Probability and trigger	Degree and distribution of danger	Recommended action in back country
Low (green)	Natural avalanches very unlikely. Human triggered avalanches unlikely. Generally stable snow. Isolated areas of instability.	Travel is generally safe. Normal caution advised.
Moderate (yellow)	Natural avalanches unlikely. Human triggered avalanches possible. Unstable slabs possible on steep terrain.	Use caution in steeper terrain.
Considerable (orange)	Natural avalanches possible. Human triggered avalanches probable. Unstable slabs probable on steep terrain.	Be increasingly cautious in steeper terrain.
High (red)	Natural and human triggered avalanches likely. Unstable slabs likely on a variety of aspects and slope angles.	Travel in avalanche terrain is not recommended. Safest travel on windward ridges of lower angle slopes without steeper terrain above.
Extreme (red/black border)	Widespread natural or human triggered avalanches certain. Extremely unstable slabs certain on most aspects and slope angles. Large destructive avalanches possible.	Travel in avalanche terrain should be avoided and confined to low angle terrain well away from avalanche path run-outs.

EUROPEAN AVALANCHE DANGER SCALE

The following scale is used in Europe.

Degree of hazard	Snowpack stability	Avalanche probability
1 (low)	The snowpack is generally well bonded and stable.	Triggering is possible only with high additional loads on a few very steep extreme slopes. Only a few small natural avalanches (sluffs) possible.
2 (moderate)	The snowpack is moderately well bonded on some steep slopes, otherwise generally well bonded.	Triggering is possible with high additional loads, particularly on the steep slopes indicated in the bulletin. Large natural avalanches not likely.
3 (considerable)	The snowpack is moderately to weakly bonded on many steep slopes.	Triggering is possible, sometimes even with low additional loads. The bulletin may indicate many slopes, which are particularly affected. In certain conditions, medium and occasionally large sized natural avalanches may occur.
4 (high)	The snowpack is weakly bonded in most places.	Triggering is probable even with low additional loads on many steep slopes. In some conditions, frequent medium or large sized natural avalanches are likely.
5 (very high)	The snowpack is generally weakly bonded and largely unstable.	Numerous large natural avalanches are likely, even on moderately steep terrain

MOUNTAIN WALKING AND TREKKING

This book is ideal for novices and experienced walkers alike, including everything you need to know about navigating hills and mountains. It includes a section on weather, from interpreting charts to dealing with a thunderstorm, tells you how to prepare for your trek, including packing your rucksack, and demystifies the art of scrambling and climbing Via ferrata safely.

RUCKSACK GUIDE
MOUNTAIN WALKING
AND TREKKING

alun richardson

ROCK CLIMBING

Rock climbing can be a tough, sometimes dangerous, physical and mental challenge. This book covers everything you need to know to be safe when ascending steep rock formations, including belaying, aid climbing and how to learn to move efficiently.

RUCKSACK GUIDE
ROCK CLIMBING

alun richardson

MOUNTAINEERING IN REMOTE AREAS OF THE WORLD

This is the essential handbook for planning and undertaking mountaineering expeditions around the world. It offers concise guidance, including where to go and when, advice on dangerous animals, minimising your impact on the environment, and dealing with extreme situations.

ALPINISM

Venturing to the Alps for the first time can be daunting. This volume covers everything you need to know about ascending these magnificent mountains, in summer and winter.

SKI MOUNTAINEERING AND SNOWSHOEING

Mountaineering on skis or snowshoes requires the ability to ski off-piste, good navigation skills, and awareness of the risks of the mountain environment in winter – you will find all of the above and more covered in this handbook.